crime and risk

```
compact
criminology
```

Compact Criminology is an exciting new series that invigorates and challenges the international field of criminology.

Books in the series are short, authoritative, innovative assessments of emerging issues in criminology and criminal justice – offering critical, accessible introductions to important topics. They take a global rather than a narrowly national approach. Eminently readable and first-rate in quality, each book is written by a leading specialist.

Compact Criminology provides a new type of tool for teaching and research, one that is flexible and light on its feet. The series is designed to address fundamental needs in the growing and increasingly differentiated field of criminology.

Other *Compact Criminology* titles include:

Comparing Criminal Justice by David Nelken
Crime and Risk by Pat O'Malley
Crime and Terrorism by Peter Grabosky and Michael Stohl
Experimental Criminology by Lawrence Sherman

crime and risk

Pat O'Malley

Los Angeles | London | New Delhi
Singapore | Washington DC

First published 2010

Apart from any fair dealing for the purposes of research
or private study, or criticism or review, as permitted
under the Copyright, Designs and Patents Act, 1988, this
publication may be reproduced, stored or transmitted in any
form, or by any means, only with the prior permission in
writing of the publishers, or in the case of reprographic
reproduction, in accordance with the terms of licences
issued by the Copyright Licensing Agency. Enquiries
concerning reproduction outside those terms should be
sent to the publishers.

SAGE Publications Ltd
1 Oliver's Yard
55 City Road
London EC1Y 1SP

SAGE Publications Inc.
2455 Teller Road
Thousand Oaks, California 91320

SAGE Publications India Pvt Ltd
B 1/I 1 Mohan Cooperative Industrial Area
Mathura Road, New Delhi 110 044
India

SAGE Publications Asia-Pacific Pte Ltd
33 Pekin Street #02-01
Far East Square
Singapore 048763

Library of Congress Control Number 2009938436

British Library Cataloguing in Publication data

A catalogue record for this book is available from the British Library

ISBN 978-1-84787-350-7 (hbk)
ISBN 978-1-84787-351-4 (pbk)

Typeset by C&M Digitals (P) Ltd, Chennai, India
Printed by CPI Antony Rowe, Chippenham, Wiltshire
Printed on paper from sustainable resources

contents

acknowledgements

I would like to thank the editors of this series, Nicole Rafter and Paul Rock, for their positive, insightful and exceptionally prompt comments on various drafts of this book. Caroline Porter of Sage Publications was a pleasure to work with and unfailingly supportive. Parts of the final chapter draw from an earlier paper 'Experiments in risk and criminal justice' published in *Theoretical Criminology* 12(4). I would like to thank the editors and Sage Publications as publishers of this journal for allowing me this licence.

ONE

risk, crime and criminal justice

Risk and crime control

Beginning about the mid-1980s, criminologists began remarking on the ways in which the governance of crime – from policing and crime prevention to sentencing and prison organization – had moved away from a focus on reforming offenders toward preventing crime and managing behaviour using predictive techniques. Some noted that whereas the principal concern of twentieth-century 'penal modernism' had been to understand and scientifically correct offenders, increasingly that was being abandoned in favour of focusing on managing their behaviours (Cohen 1985, Simon 1988). No-one was much interested anymore in the motives and meanings of these people. Instead what was at issue was what they did, how to control them, and how to minimize the harms they generated. Offenders and their offences were coming to be reframed less as the pathological products of societal and psychological breakdowns who needed to be therapeutically reformed, and more as bundles of harmful behaviours and potentialities.

At the same time, other criminologists observed that new techniques and new concerns were emerging in crime control. Reflecting the focus on behaviours, they detected a new emphasis on shaping the environment, and especially the built environment, in order to make crime difficult or impossible (Shearing and Stenning 1985, Reichman 1986). Increasingly, crime was seen as a matter of people taking opportunities rather than in terms of their inappropriate attitudes or disadvantaged backgrounds. Crime prevention accordingly was moving away from building up supportive environments and improving economically deprived neighbourhoods. The new focus was increasingly on designing crime-proof buildings, crime-preventing streetscapes and communities. As David Garland (1996) was later to term it, interest was focused on 'criminogenic situations'. Reducing the risk of crime by restricting criminal opportunities had become critical.

There were other, linked changes also being reported. Penal modernism – the optimistic correctional approach that deployed scientific knowledge in order to reform offenders – was vitally interested in offenders' pasts in order that they could be understood as individuals. The emerging risk techniques in crime control were also interested in offenders' pasts, but in a different way. Emerging techniques tended to use statistical methods to identify correlations between pre-existing conditions and criminal action and to treat these conditions as 'risk factors'. These factors could be used especially to identify potential offenders and change their ways before they offended, rather than correcting them after offending. Furthermore, what was now of interest was to use such information to assign individuals to a certain risk pool: it was this risk-categorization rather than the unique individual that was of interest.

This had been a phenomenally successful model in the medical sciences, of course. By the 1970s it was already the case that all manner of afflictions could be detected in advance by the presence of certain risk factors such as fatty diet and sedentary lifestyle, a family history of certain cancers or heart disease and so on. By modifying our diet and lifestyle, taking drugs or in extreme cases undergoing precautionary surgery, those of us identified as 'at risk' may ward off some dreaded cancer or debilitating disease. Over the last half century, almost every aspect of our lives has been affected by this ascendant risk model of government. The design of cars, planes, roads, buildings and household equipment; the shaping of our bodies both inside and out; the production and consumption of food and clothing; patterns of saving and investment; education and training – all these and more are now 'governed by risk'. And why not? Who would not wish to reduce their exposure to disease, injury, loss or premature death? Who would not want to mitigate financial harms through some form of insurance? Perhaps it is not surprising that, sooner or later, crime would come to be approached in the same way. In fact it's surprising that risk management techniques came to crime control so late in the piece, for contiguous fields such as fire prevention had been developed on similar principles almost a century earlier.

By the end of the twentieth century, risk had become a predominant way of governing all manner of problems. Prevention is better than cure. Of course it is true that even with respect to governing health through risk techniques there are political and moral dilemmas. Many people refuse to control their smoking or diet on the basis of a personal preference. The introduction of seat belts met with some resistance as an infringement on personal freedom. Fluoridation of the water supply to prevent tooth decay created pockets of alarm and protest. Yet for the most part, these were objections focused on specific issues, and were short lived, individual or local struggles. The model of risk itself – the use of predictive statistical knowledge linked to techniques of harm prevention – overwhelmingly has been regarded as one of the benefits bestowed by science. However, with respect to the governance of crime, this is not altogether how things have gone, and especially not in criminology.

Broadly speaking a fissure has opened up that divides opinion across almost the whole range of criminological and penological concerns – legislation, crime prevention, policing, sentencing, prison regimes and post-release interventions. On one side are those who take a generally positive view of risk techniques. Frequently those supportive of the use of risk techniques work in psychology and related disciplines, and/or in government offices, police and correctional agencies and institutions. On the face of things their views are not unreasonable. They seek to reduce crime victimization, to lower the public cost of crime, to deflect individuals from a life of crime and punishment, and to use risk techniques to provide services to reduce the risk of prisoners reoffending. Set against these so-called 'administrative criminologists' are their traditional foes – a great number of academic criminologists and certainly most of those coming from critical criminology and social justice disciplines. The warring camps will be depressingly familiar to anyone with even a passing knowledge of criminology, for they are traditional enemies. But why has risk become another of their interminable battlegrounds? And why do increasing numbers of lawyers and judges voice concerns with, and opposition to, risk-based crime prevention?

For critical criminologists, by the late 1990s, risk-based approaches were seen to have played a key role in the emergence of the 'culture of control' in which the reformist and socially inclusive optimism of modernist penal policies has been submerged beneath an exclusionary and punitive approach to crime. Because of its focus on behaviour rather than therapeutic correction, and on offenders as risks to others rather than as disadvantaged people struggling with the challenges of life, the new risk techniques were seen by critics to mesh well with an emerging 'new punitiveness' (Garland 2001, Pratt et al. 2005). Examples that support this view are not hard to find. This is not only because they erode 'progressive' reformism in criminal justice, but also because they have often become high-profile political issues in the media and public consciousness. For example, 'three strikes and you're out' and similar tariff-based sentencing policies focus on the risk that an offender represents rather than on the seriousness of the particular offence at issue. For quite minor offences – but offences that are seen to be part of a pattern of activity that indicates a high risk of future crime – offenders can be imprisoned for long periods. These approaches to sentencing collide with almost taken-for-granted principles of proportionality between wrong and punishment, for a relatively minor offence may result in a lengthy risk-based sentence. They also fly in the face of therapeutic thinking that sentences should reflect the correctional needs of the offender as judged by experts.

Other examples exist in abundance. Curfews imposed on troublesome teenagers and electronic tagging of sex offenders in the name of risk reduction, are condemned as doing nothing to reform the offender while limiting the freedom of many people whose offences are minor. They are also viewed as turning the community into an extension of the prison system. Another prominent instance includes 'Megan's Laws' and 'Sarah's Laws', where in the name of risk minimization the identities and often the addresses of former sex and violence offenders are made public. The stated aim is to warn people in the neighbourhood to take extra precautions in view of this risk in their midst. These laws have become associated with accusations that they promote vigilantism and victimization of past offenders who may be trying to reform themselves or whose offences may in fact be quite mild. They may also create living hells for the families of the offenders.

Such ways of using risk to reduce crime are viewed as extending punishment into an indefinite future after release from prison, and as making unbearable the lives of former offenders and their families without this technique actually being proven to reduce crime victimization (Levi 2000). On top of this, a 'new penology' based on risk is seen to be shifting emphasis from correction to risk-reducing incapacitation or warehousing (Feeley and Simon 1992, 1994). A prime example is taken to be the imprisonment of many of those incarcerated under 'three strikes' laws, who are imprisoned in the name of reducing risk to the community but who receive little or nothing by way of correctional services while they are inside. The goal is simply to remove these 'risks' from society.

Alongside these changes, crime prevention moved from the margins to the centre of policing activities. Many of these new developments have been regarded by criminologists as deeply troubling. Reducing crime opportunities by creating 'gated communities', and the widespread installation of closed circuit television (CCTV) to monitor public spaces, are seen to create a paranoid society. In this view, intervening against the different, the unwanted and the merely annoying is a principal means whereby we are creating an 'exclusive security' (Young 1999). Pre-emptive intervention against 'pre-delinquents' and 'at risk' young people, 'threatening' gangs of youths or 'anti-social' groups of teenagers congregating in shopping malls inflict restrictions on those who may not yet have done anything dangerous or illegal. Crime awareness campaigns aimed at improving public safety are often regarded as increasing the sense of insecurity and adversely affecting the quality of life for all citizens. Such problematic and often worrying developments are viewed by critics as exemplary of risk techniques' *characteristic* forms. In what has become a new orthodoxy in critical criminology, risk appears overwhelmingly as a negative development in crime control and criminal justice, driving out the inclusive model of criminal correction and installing in our midst segregating practices and technologies.

Such critical criminological views reflect social theory's abiding pessimism about the present. It is epitomized by works such as Bauman's (2000) and Young's (1999) sociologies of the 'exclusive society' and Agamben's (2000, 2005) apocalyptic vision of the state of exception.

For Agamben, those who pose threats to security are consigned to a vulnerable form of humanity increasingly stripped of the rights and protections others take for granted, living a life deemed not worthy of living. In these accounts, criminal justice, public security and social exclusion blur together, and in the post-9/11, post-social-welfare state there seems little hope of change except for the worse. It is hard to disagree with many of the points they make, substantiated as they are by copious research.

However, these analyses pick up and maybe over-emphasize just one trend, albeit a powerful one, and they rarely suggest any way out of the nightmare they depict. I will argue that there are other trends and other possibilities with respect to risk. These include 'developmental crime prevention' and some forms of 'risk-needs' service provisions in prisons in which social reform programs and/or individual treatment are provided where a crime prevention risk-reducing effect can be demonstrated. Of course, as David Garland (2001) argues, these can be regarded as part of the culture of control, for they subordinate correctional reform and social assistance to techniques of crime prevention. As this implies, they will only be provided for offenders and the needy to the extent that they are shown to reduce crime risks.

This is a valid and important point. But they can also be seen as sites of resistance by the 'social' professions – psychologists, social workers, psychiatrists and so on seeking to maintain or defend the welfare orientations and the therapeutic corrections that so many criminologists complain are being swept away. More significantly, they can be seen as points from which more promising initiatives can be explored or launched. In this way they are possibly Janus-faced, offering at least *ambiguous* risk-based alternatives to the apparently desolate culture of control. 'Drug harm minimization' is likewise dangerous but promising. As will be seen, it offers therapeutic services and efforts to reintegrate and accommodate drug users in society in the name of reducing the total array of harms illicit drug use creates. On the other hand, it does impose expert domination and subjects therapeutic services to the test of reducing those actions and behaviours judged by experts to be harmful and risk-laden. It also has the potential to extend the net of social control, for example by the use of methadone programs as a 'chemical leash' for users. Whatever their other benefits, methadone programs are intrusive and constraining, requiring users to report at frequent intervals to an approved drug agency, and often making them submit urine tests to detect illicit drug use. All of these risk-related formations have dangerous potentials. People who have not been convicted of an offence are required to restrict their movements, be available to surveillance and provide personal information. But they may also offer the potential for the reconfiguring of risk in more optimistic, socially inclusive and constructive fashion than is imagined by many of those opposed to crime control through risk techniques. Perhaps it is time, in the twenty-first century, to explore this 'uncertain promise' of risk.

Risk and criminal activity

At the same time, and with the same guarded optimism, it is also important to explore the ways in which social theory can reframe risk with respect to understanding the motives and ways of life that lie behind criminal offending. Positivist criminology has long attended to crime as risk-taking. Usually, it does so in a way that regards risk-taking as pathological. Thus 'short-term hedonism' produced by poor socialization, or 'thrill seeking' produced by the boredom of lower-class working life, are ideas that have been deployed by positivist criminologists (e.g. Miller 1958). These approaches tend to reduce risk-taking to the status of a problem leading to crime, and to attribute it to personal inadequacy and social malaise. This vision is in many ways a remnant of the nineteenth-century view of the poor as feckless, lacking proper prudence and needing an injection of discipline.

Such criminological work can readily be accused of class bias. For example, while some criminologists see crime arising from risk-taking as a response to the boring lives of workers, it is hard to believe that the lives of many white-collar males (including criminologists) are startlingly different when it comes to day-to-day excitement. Indeed, evidence abounds of white-collar workers engaging in binge drinking and illicit drug consumption on the night club circuit (Winlow and Hall 2006). Furthermore, this pathologizing approach to crime as risk-taking is associated with treatment responses to teach better impulse control and deferred gratification. Consequently it can be accused of seeking to make the poor and especially the young modify their ways in order to conform to the moral standards of the middle classes and the requirements of public order bureaucrats. Other pathologizing criminological models, such as that of Hans Eysenck (1978) suggest that some people are driven to risk-taking because of problems with their autonomic nervous system. People with a 'slow' or unresponsive nervous system are believed to require more stimulus in order to provide levels of satisfaction. Such 'extraverted' individuals are driven to more 'extreme' activities – such as risk-taking – that have a high probability of being associated with crime. Of course, the same is seen to be true for sky divers, arctic explorers and many great achievers – and to be fair to Eysenck and his allies, they do recognize that risk-taking is also socially productive.

Sophisticated variants of this kind of criminology go on to argue that working-class risk-taking is linked to crime largely because there are fewer legitimate outlets for excitement open to the poor. Yet even such approaches still carry with them a baggage of determinism that many critical criminologists find problematic: an assumption that certain people are driven to crime by something in their bodies or their background. Against this kind of approach to risk-taking it is argued in ways epitomized by Jack Katz's (1988) *Seductions of Crime,* that the experience of risk can be analysed as a form of resistance and creativity. Common-or-garden shoplifting, for example, is too widespread across class lines to be explained in conventional terms as either the poor attempting to eke out a living or as evidence of the working classes trying to escape from the tedium of factory jobs. Katz explores the experiential phenomenology of such activities rather than trying to reduce them to an effect of some determining variable. He attempts to render these experiences intelligible as a form of risky flirting with the humiliation of capture that generates 'sneaky thrills', and thus provide excitement available to all. Perhaps the children of the middle class, standing to lose more, would find this even more thrilling, no matter how supposedly less boring their lives are than those of their working-class peers.

Some crime therefore can be understood as 'embracing risk', to use Baker and Simon's (2002) term. Such crimes may emerge as not needing a pathological, determinist explanation. After all, the current world of consumer culture constitutes excitement as good, as normal and as desirable. Risk-takers who end up committing crimes in pursuit of excitement may thus embrace actions that embody mainstream values. Perhaps their misfortune, and their main difference from other people, is not their background or their nervous system, but that they choose to seek excitement and risk-taking in what is judged to be a 'subterranean', inconvenient or 'inappropriate' fashion (Matza 1964).

The work of 'cultural criminologists' and others has extended this work more recently, linking legally problematic risk-taking to broader themes extolling the virtues of risk-taking in contemporary consumer society. Key examples include writings on 'edgework' – for example extreme sports such as base-jumping (parachuting off cliffs or illegally off high rise structures), or the criminal financial speculation that has blossomed in the morally ambiguous cultural milieu of risk-taking created by the 'enterprise society'. However, even while exhibiting continuities with mainstream values of embracing risk, some criminal risk-taking may be seen as intertwined with resistance to a perceived dominant culture and agencies of authority. While it is easy to slip into romanticizing and patronizing in this way, nevertheless the act of resistance is often itself exhilarating through the risks it bears – even if this takes complex forms of fear, anger, arrogance and even cruelty.

This kind of personal orientation to risk and excitement is not necessarily new. Yet perhaps the expansion of consumer culture, coupled with the neo-liberal political emphasis on risk-taking as valued attribute in the 'entrepreneurial' society, combine to produce an environment in which crimes embracing risk become more attractive to many people, especially young people. At the same time, legitimate forms of risky consumption – such as 'lifestyle choices' associated with certain styles of dress and music, bodily adornment and attending night clubs and casinos – may have become more 'edgy'. That is, in the culture and environment of the consumer society, the boundary between legitimate and illegitimate is becoming more volatile or ambiguous. Resistance and flirting with crime even becomes a theme in many legitimate commodities ranging from alcopops to motorbikes. Perhaps here too, 'risk' offers uncertain lines of flight out of a present that many commentators and young people alike see as being rendered unfree by a political over-emphasis on security. The allegedly hegemonic 'culture of control' seems to leave little room for resistance, yet risk-taking may be one of the key forms of such potentially transformative activity paradoxically generated by different facets of neoliberal, consumer society.

What may be particularly characteristic of the present era is that a heightened emphasis on risk-taking is colliding with a heightened emphasis on risk-containment. In other words, there have been risk-managing forms of government before now, but they have not been so pervasive, so sophisticated and so politically and culturally salient. Likewise, there have been plenty of examples of risk-taking crimes in the past, but perhaps now risk-taking has become much more widespread and so much more a part of everyday life. As a result more people, and especially more young people, are attracted to styles of living and to activities that have risk-taking as a key part of their make-up. Life may have become more exciting! Or at least there are more opportunities for excitement embedded in the everyday life of consumer society; they are evaluated differently, and more people are interested in taking advantage of them.

But to the extent that this is true, it is on a collision course with a governing focus that makes risk-taking more of a problem and that has developed more and more ways of regulating through risk-management techniques. These intervene in the interstices of everyday life and are more sensitive to 'risky' behaviour than previous ways of governing. In such an environment, especially one served so thoroughly by mass media hungry for spectacle and all too ready to report new 'shocks and horrors', everyone becomes more risk conscious. Borrowing from the old idea of 'deviancy amplification' (for example, Young 1974) in which actions beget social reactions which tend to exaggerate the difference of the initial action, we could speculate that we are caught up in a risk spiral. Perhaps more and more of life's experiences, both of the governed and the governing, are understood and experienced in terms of risk. And perhaps that spiral is pushing us toward something new. Certainly not necessarily all good, but not necessarily all as bad as risk theorists and the culture of control suggests. Just new, different, and as the future always is, full of potentials we can only guess at.

Approaches to risk and crime

For various commentators, all this emphasis on risk, whether as embracing or minimizing risk, reflects a society that has become risk obsessed. For the influential German theorist Ulrich Beck (1992, 1997, 2002), the current environment is characterized by 'risk consciousness'. From top to bottom, from international government to the ways private individuals govern their lives, we are said to think in terms of risks because the world has become a more risky place. It is not simply that there are more risks, for example associated with mundane matters such as the growth of towns and the massively increased use of the automobile. Rather, Beck's concerns are with global 'modernization risks' that are generated out of the unholy marriage of capitalism and technology. These threaten the survival of our species. Global warming, holes in the ozone layer, global financial crises, swine flu, nuclear contamination and the threat of nuclear holocaust are examples of catastrophic risks that seem to announce themselves without warning.

Because technological development is accelerated by capitalist desire for profit, it is said to advance faster than the means to register its potential harmful effects. Because governments are complicit in promoting technological and economic growth it is argued that the capacity to harm escaped democratic regulation long ago. We are reduced to picking up the pieces long after most of the damage has been done, or only brought to act when we are already well down the slippery slope to catastrophe. Such disastrous potentialities usually exist on the margins of scientific understanding, leading to a new era of disputes between experts over what is to be done. Ongoing disputes over greenhouse gas emissions are just one example. Yet the world's peoples are all affected by the reach of these threats. Indeed, as an effect of the global and unpredictable nature of such risks, many traditional risk-management institutions – national governments, trades unions, nuclear families – become obsolete. Unable to cope with these new threats, they are said to be hollowed out or dismantled, leaving individuals more exposed to risk.

Ironically, in the face of the unpredictable nature of this new risky and 'uncertain' world, and confronted by an associated decline in faith in expertise, the demand for risk-based security increases exponentially as the sense of insecurity balloons out of hand. Equally ironically, the more that risk becomes the framework for dealing with problems, the more that new risks are revealed, thus generating further heightening of risk consciousness and a vicious circle of fear and securitization. It is a condition that many (for example, Ericson and Haggerty 1998) see as affecting the ways in which crime has become a much more prominent issue needing to be governed by new risk techniques.

This is yet another sociological nightmare scenario, and like so much of its kind it reduces the problems of existence to a single grand contradiction in historical development. There are many problems confronting this kind of theoretical analysis. Distrust of experts is not new nor is fundamental disagreement between them. Much of the demand for risk-based security can be traced to its demonstrated effectiveness in areas such as health, engineering and so on, rather than to catastrophic dangers created by out of control science and technology. Little or no evidence is produced to indicate that risk consciousness is as generalized or as novel as is claimed. Most of all, can we plausibly attribute such diverse phenomena as changes in family structure, early-warning testing for cancer, holes in the ozone layer, international terrorism, the changing (and disputed) fortunes of the nation state and the demand for increased security against crime – let alone the interest in risk-taking – to a single development? Maybe this has a political function, for it is explicitly a call to arms that makes for broad mobilization because of its seeming power to explain so much. But even if it is right, does it offer useful ways of thinking about crime and crime control in the twenty-first century? Or is it too abstract, or too vague and general to account for what is going on in such specific fields?

Nevertheless, some influential criminologists have tied their analyses to this model. For example Ericson and Haggerty's (1998) analysis uses exactly this theory to explain why and how contemporary policing has been transformed by risk consciousness, risk institutions (notably insurance) and risk techniques. Hebenton and Thomas' (1996) work likewise has used Ulrich Beck's approach to understand the current focus on the risk management associated with sex-offender laws. Both of these will be discussed in the next chapter. But other approaches are available that might not share the same kinds of difficulty created by using such a grand theory to explain rather specific phenomena.

Risk and governmentality

For the most part, analyses of risk and criminal justice have preferred rather more modest theoretical schemes. Probably the most influential framework for understanding risk minimization has been that of governmentality, an approach that maps out the techniques and rationalities in terms of which government takes place. For example, crime prevention can be understood as shaped by the political turn toward neo-liberalism with its stress on cost-effective governance, in which framework prevention is regarded as more effective than punishment after the event. This governmentality approach is rather hostile to 'grand theories', preferring to focus on the contingent and specific turns of history and politics. The prominence of risk appears as something emerging out of a variety of developments that follow no course set out by some motor of history such as the forces and relations of production, or that appears as the effect of a grand transformation of modernity such as Beck envisages. In this way, governmentality tends to see the present as contingent, and the future therefore as open and malleable. Things needn't be as they are now – hence the future too appears as more open to political possibilities. It is also an approach that is more at ease than most theories with the uncertainties and ambiguities in the way events occur.

By destabilizing the present in this way, and avoiding visions of unfolding historical logics or contradictions, governmentality seems to me to have considerable potential for optimism about changing the future, even if some of its practitioners do not emphasize this aspect. In keeping with this contingent view of history, governmentality is much more concerned to map out the diversity of risk-based approaches to government, and their distinct genealogies, than to collapse them all into one unified category of risk or risk society. For example, writers in the risk society tradition are little concerned about differences between the risk model of public health oriented drug harm minimization and the aggressive and criminalizing risk models (such as workplace and school drug testing) used by the War on Drugs. As both reflect a risk-focus, they are seen to fit with that theory. But clearly their political implications, their implications for crime control, and their implications for the lives of drug users, are significantly different. Governmentality on the other hand is closely concerned with the different implications of these various configurations of risk with respect to the way we are governed. It focuses on the kinds of subjects government programs wish to make us into – for example, irrational 'drug addicts' versus rational but drug-dependent 'drug users'. It makes central the specific techniques through which such subjects are controlled and shaped, such as needle and syringe exchanges versus compulsory detox facilities. And it attempts to make clear the costs to our lives of being imagined and moulded in such divergent ways. It is precisely because of its strengths in these respects that this book will largely adopt governmentality with respect to understanding risk in criminal justice.

This is not intended to imply that governmentality can help only in the understanding of 'state' government programs, such as those of criminal justice. 'Government' in this approach refers to any way of shaping conduct, right down to the ways in which shopping centres try to govern young people's 'loitering', or individuals try to govern their lives by subjecting themselves to certain risk regimes, such as making their homes more secure against crime (O'Malley 1991). Nor, of course, does it imply that only risk-*minimizing* governance is its subject. Jonathan Simon (2002), for example, has used governmentality to understand how the rise of 'extreme sports' can be linked to governmental programs of neo-liberalism and their stress on risk-taking as enriching (in all senses of the word). As noted above, this broad political rationality generates a cultural milieu in which risk-taking may be regarded as a 'good thing' and be applied to all manner of domains other than those originally imagined. In the nineteenth century, prudence had been such a strong requirement imposed on the mass by Victorian liberal politics, that risk-taking was generally frowned upon except among a privileged few who could afford this luxury. Rich stock market investors, explorers, military heroes, missionaries might all have been approved risk-takers, although in each case their qualification and domain of action was tightly circumscribed. Nowadays (even after the 2008–09 global financial meltdown) we are all supposed to be 'entrepreneurs' of our own lives, to take risks on our own behalf and so on. Therefore it is not surprising when investment bankers pick up such approved ideas and apply them in a 'subterranean' fashion to investment activities that come to be defined as criminally reckless (Smith 2005). One way of looking at this would be to say that the neo-liberal governmental rationality has been 'innovated' into legally problematic practices by certain individuals or groups. Governmentality may be useful as a way of rendering intelligible the risky rationalities deployed by such individuals and groups, and the ambiguities of their relations with other rationalities such as neo-liberalism as developed in parliamentary contexts.

Cultural approaches to risk and crime

At this point we touch on a third critical approach to risk. It is one that provides an important bridge linking risk-minimizing and risk-taking: the 'cultural theory' associated with the work of Mary Douglas (Douglas 1992, Lupton 1999). With respect to risk-taking, a cultural approach emphasizes the diverse meanings and valuations of risk held by individuals and groups. For example, it would regard the rational choice actor model – focusing on how individuals 'rationally calculate' the odds of risky behaviour being rewarding – as *one* cultural meaning of risk. It is, for example, a model favoured by economists, but just because of that fact, it is still a 'cultural' construct. This can be contrasted with other ways of constituting risk culturally. For example, young offenders may regard such a rational way of calculating risk as a sign of weakness and lack of guts, or the way in which the conventional world thinks – a world they despise and want to get away from. 'Spontaneity' and emotion become much more important in some of these cultural visions which reject the intellectual world that rational calculation represents. Linked to this, young offenders may so highly rate the value in status terms of some particular illegal action, or so value the immediacy and impact of a thrill delivered by risk-taking itself, that a calculation of their likely capture never crosses their minds.

For this third approach, risk is a cultural product – to be understood as inextricably bound up with questions of value. Risk emerges not just as a particular configuration of techniques, nor as the effect of a grand unfolding of modern contradictions between science and survival, but as a matter of lived experiences, emotionally laden evaluations, expressions of inchoate feelings and so on. Such cultural considerations inform not only what are to be considered the 'acceptable' levels of risk, or what risks are worth taking, or even what risks are worth minimizing, but also whether something should be allowed to be dealt with as a 'risk' at all. Pregnancy is an example where all of these value positions and the debates they engender are highly salient in the current environment.

While almost self-evidently useful with respect to understanding risk-taking crimes, this cultural approach to risk has been comparatively little used with respect to criminal justice. Yet as Garland has argued (1991), one of criminology's blind spots – perhaps one that governmentality falls into too – is not being able to theorize or think about emotional responses to crime and the way these shape governance. Governmentality might help us to see how something like Megan's Law represents a risk-based response to crime, by attending to their official justifications and the techniques used. But such laws also emerge from a groundswell of emotion, of fear and loathing, that is better understood in terms of the 'popular' experiences, beliefs and expressions that do not appear in formal legal rationalities. As Jonathan Simon (1998) argues, these laws are not simply about risk, but at least equally about outrage and vengeance.

In this way, it can readily be seen that there is no necessary hiatus between governmentality and cultural approaches to risk, for the latter provide insight into the value bases out of which the governmental rationalities and technologies of risk are produced, or that create an environment in which they receive political support. Cultural approaches to risk can bring to the analysis of crime and crime control dimensions that are often regarded as alien or external to governmentality. In particular, these include an emphasis on examining the culturally shaped experience of risk, including fear of crime and the ways in which risk-taking as a culturally meaningful activity emerges out of the sheer desire for thrills or a hatred of criminal justice authorities.

Governmentality's strength may also be a weakness. It is far more interested in plans and programs rather than in their implementations or in the ways in which those governed respond to them. But this can lead to a rather rigid and static image of things. Resistance and re-interpretation generate change, whether through obstructing govern-ance or through changing and adapting it to other purposes. Rather than seeing governance only through the eyes of the programmers, as is the preference of governmentality, cultural approaches emphasize the experiential dimension. Risk-taking, especially, may be understood as an aspect of governmental programs, but it can also be understood as a pleasurable experience, as exciting, and such emotional experiences can be part of the 'seduction' of crime. This is also the legacy of Katz's (1988) work, for example on the 'sneaky thrills' of shoplifting.

For such reasons, cultural criminology itself may be seen as incorporating a cultural approach to risk. I am not suggesting that somehow governmentality is 'incomplete' because it does not address issues of emotionality or 'direct experience' in such ways. Governmentality is not intended to address questions of experience or emotionality and needs no 'completion' of this sort. But as one aim of this book is to bring together crime control as risk management *and* crime as risk-taking, then an approach such as cultural criminology seems self-evidently useful. Thus in the third chapter, I will rely increasingly on the analyses and kinds of investigation favoured by Katz and his successor cultural criminologists such as Ferrel and his colleagues (Ferrell et al. 2004, Presdee 2000, Young 1999, 2007, Hayward 2004). Such work pays great attention to the ways in which crime is experienced and made sense of by, among others, offenders, mass media, victims, police and the public. Its stress on the cultural meanings generated in and around criminality, especially in consumer societies, make clear that cultural criminology does not require a governmentality to be melded with it – any more than vice versa. However, the two are quite complementary in their coverage of the governance of the constituted meanings of crime. Governmentality can bring to cultural criminological work a tried and useful way of dissecting and understanding the nature, forms and implications of governing regimes that seek to govern crime 'through' risk.

It is worth stressing that these two approaches, governmentality and cultural criminology, both emphasize the open-ended, arbitrary and socially constructed nature of the subject matter of social theory. Both approaches adopt a generally critical political stance. Both seem to me to sit well with a politics that does not set out a theoretically driven social program that must be followed in order that we be 'properly' free. They are at ease with a more open and experimental politics – a point that will become important toward the end of this book. Last but not least, there seems nothing in either approach that precludes them being joined together in one analysis. Current work in governmentality regards it as an analytic tool, part of a toolbox available to social theorists, rather than as a theoretical framework (Rose et al. 2006). Within limits there is no reason why it cannot be used with other tools such as are provided by cultural criminology and cultural approaches to risk. Significant lines of work in cultural criminology trace their roots to symbolic interaction and labelling theory of the 1960s, and in this way, like governmentality, are averse to grand theoretical explanations. Both could be brought together in a more open and even optimistic criminology that regards risk and risk-taking as never fixed, always changing and with potentials that are not yet known.

It could be anticipated that the hardest test of such optimism would be the burgeoning field of biocriminology. In the 1970s, many criminologists responded to Eysenck's resurrection of biological approaches to criminology with disdain and sometimes ridicule, especially as these were associated with discredited racist ideas fostered by Lombroso in the nineteenth century and by the eugenic movement and Nazi criminology of the earlier twentieth century. However, by the early 1990s alarm was beginning to spread, especially with the rise of more sophisticated genetic and neurogenetic approaches. For some (for example, Duster 1990), this had the potential to create a new preventive eugenics of crime. In one of the most influential responses, Nelken and Lindee (1995) regarded the rise of genetic approaches to crime as consigning offenders – and more problematically 'pre-offenders' – to a genetically determined life course from which they could not escape. As a corollary, they assumed that risk-based interception and incapacitation would displace reform and reintegration and the welfare orientations of penal modernism – the culture of control would never be reined in. Again, risk appears as part of the forces driving, rather than being shaped by, the broader framework of the government of crime. In science fiction, works such as Phillip Kerr's (1996) A *Philosophical Investigation* fanned the flames, with his vision of a 'Lombroso program' which could use DNA to identify and control pre-killers.

In practice, however, almost no genetics researchers envisaged any such possibility, arguing instead that genetic determinism would never produce anything like a gene for crime, inter alia because of the social construction of criminal law. While, for example, there may be links between genetics and violent or aggressive behaviours, the overwhelming tendency was to see genetic factors as creating 'susceptibilities' rather than acting as determinants (Rose 2008: 244–7). In this much more conditional framework, emphasis is put most heavily on what kinds of interventions and techniques of the self can reduce or ameliorate the risks of offending. Immediately, the temptation is to leap to an incapacitation model. This is by no means the only possibility: it *is* a possibility – and a very strong possibility – where the culture of control is unchecked, but at least equally possible, and at least as readily identifiable among the current programmatic responses to biocriminology, have been therapeutic responses much along the lines of the welfare sanctions of 30 years ago. Thus Rose (2000) emphasizes that 'the contemporary biologization of risky identities in the name of public health offers biological criminologists a role as therapeutic professionals'. Again, this may not always be the ideal course. It is itself risky and dangerous, creating opportunities for technocratic domination, but it also creates new possibilities for some more positive interventions than incapacitation and incarceration. Risk itself is not the problem.

In sum, as Nicole Rafter (2008: 246) has argued, the problem of biocriminology 'lies not with the scientists who are investigating biological causes of crime but rather with simplistic or politically manipulative understandings of their work. To avoid the misappropriation of biocriminology for political ends … we need to learn how to question science intelligently and acknowledge our own ignorance'. More generally, I would suggest, this implies that criminologists abandon their pessimism, especially on this question, and begin to engage proactively to appropriate risk for positive initiatives, and to counter the conservative politics of control with a democratization of risk itself.

Crime, risk and excitement

It was suggested above that crime and risk management, and crime as risk-taking need to be considered together because their convergence has marked the years at least since the 1970s and probably earlier. Broadly speaking, this conjunction can be seen to emerge out of a broader contingency – the rise of consumer capitalism since World War II, and the development and ascendancy of neo-liberal politics since the 1970s.

Together, these two influences have done much to erode, or at least significantly change, the world of the closed disciplinary institutions and the ethos of self-denial and deferred gratification that characterized the period before World War II. While Margaret Thatcher (1992) liked to talk of the rediscovery of such Victorian virtues, their take-up has been restricted to matters of individual responsibility and to the valorization of competition and markets. Self-denial and self-sacrifice have not notably been embraced in everyday life and politics. The expansion of commodification in the neo-liberal period has been associated with a loosening of moral constraints so that increasingly markets cater to (and form) what have come to be called 'lifestyles' (Rose 1999). Discipline, of course, survives but increasingly is inflected by hedonism – indeed Mike Featherstone (1994) has referred to the emergent ethos as 'controlled hedonism': it is good to consume, and conspicuous consumption is the sign and reward of success. And the measure of one's success, perhaps more than ever, is high income and the possession of expensive commodities – for these are the rewards delivered by the market to those who take risks and make prosperous enterprises of their lives.

Not only does this development break down many pre-existing moral barriers, but it creates an environment of constant change, in some senses an exciting milieu in which 'all that is solid melts into air' (Berman 1983). A cultural emphasis on the value of novelty, self-gratification and expressiveness erodes or qualifies one of emotional containment and rational utilitarianism. This has created conditions for the emergence of new forms of regulation, of the sort described by Deleuze (1995) as 'control'.

In 'control societies' concern with individuals and their conformity to narrow moral precepts, and the centrality of closed disciplinary institutions, is increasingly displaced by the immanent regulation of behaviours. We might take as a crude example the imposition of taxes on cigarettes as a way of channelling behaviour away from unwanted directions. Prices 'modulate' the frequency of actions, deflect them into other areas or activities, while at the same time being an almost taken for granted aspect of everyday life. But there is more to it than this. The driver's licence, for example, is not merely a licence to drive. It is almost the required means for providing proof of age or identity, or such other details as home address, that are so frequently required to guarantee our credentials to enter this or that site, or to purchase this or that commodity (alcohol and tobacco, for example). Likewise the credit card may now be a taken for granted part of anyone's wallet. But like the driver's licence it is also a passport, at least for those domains where access is a commodity. It acts as a sign that we have good credit – we are good risks – and thus provides an impersonal and highly portable warranty of trustworthiness in a world in which life is more than ever lived and expressed through commodities. Even these instruments of access and identity are themselves commodities. We purchase the credit card and even the driver's licence – and part of their price is the cost of a series of other security checks and verifications, carried out by credit agencies, police and so on, which they embody. Unlike cash, which, as Simmel (1990 [1895]) says, is 'undifferentiated' and anonymous, each time these instruments are used, an electronic trace is left behind. They are the perfect risk-managing collateral in a consumer society that is also a society permeated by risk consciousness, for they are at one and the same time the means of access to commodities and risk-management technologies. This is why, as urban myths have it, the Mafia always pay in cash.

While constraining us in new ways, nevertheless at the same time through such means individuals are freed to 'float' morally within constraints that work through consumption and 'choice'. The boundaries of acceptability are patrolled by such devices and the principal contours of the perimeter are coming to be associated with risks created for others (Simon 1988). Within this security perimeter, a good deal of the moral restriction of the Victorian age has been eroded. Of course, in this process, there is regulation. The commodities we purchase very largely have been approved and themselves governed by a grid of risk. Safety standards and inspections filter that which appears in the market. A broad form of censorship has selected out those objects or services considered unacceptable. But the range of moral tolerance would appal the Victorian moralist.

In complex ways, crime both is shaped and helps to shape this state of affairs. Consumption has become a much more salient domain for offending, especially where associated with crimes of the risk-embracing sort. Crimes and lesser offenses associated with motor vehicles are one example, from speeding and dangerous driving to car theft and street racing. Drug consumption, graffiti, vandalism and other activities are older forms of offending that are linked to excitement that have been given new life and new prominence in consumer society. The response to these has been Janus-faced. On the one hand are those former crimes of excitement that once exercized the police, such as gambling. Very largely these have been commodified and corporatized so that now gambling is no longer a crime but a key part of those new inventions, the leisure industry and the financial services sector. Once criminal and officially despised, now gambling is highly valued as a source of employment, capital growth and state revenue (O'Malley 2004). It is assumed that, very largely, individuals should be given responsibility for their own risk management, and a paternalistic state should not interfere in pleasures that do no harm to others. In many jurisdictions, especially outside the United States, even 'illicit' drug consumption has been extensively decriminalized on similar grounds.

The risk-perimeter cuts in especially where crimes of excitement create harms or risks for others. Here the margin for tolerance has, if anything, been closed down. Through various forms of anti-social behavioural order, all manner of 'acting out' and 'thrill seeking' that may once have been ignored or at least tolerated, now fall into the penumbra of criminal justice. And of course, much of the increased tolerance applies only to those who are 'in' the market. For the vast bulk of offenders, even in this era of the culture of control, sanctions are primarily some form of risk-management in the community. Prisons are not the principal sanction. Rather, their inmates fall into two classes. First are the 'failed consumers'. These include a large number of those who cannot afford to pay fines, the consumer society penalty par excellence, and who in many jurisdictions may be imprisoned in default (O'Malley 2009a). Through much of the twentieth century they supplied up to a third or even more of prison admissions. The other principal category is made up of those who present risks of a magnitude that are deemed inappropriate to be governed through market techniques. And among these are many who present only a small risk, but, as Feeley and Simon (1992) put it, they have so little to lose that they are deemed to fall below the threshold of deterrence. But here the discussion strays back into the question of risk and criminal justice, to which we shall now turn in detail.

TWO

risk and crime control

One way of dating the appearance of risk as a major focus with respect to the governance of crime is the publication of Martinson's (1974) now notorious paper 'What Works'. Broadly speaking, it argued that after decades of correctional theory and practice, very little could be demonstrated with respect to its positive impact on reforming individuals or reducing rates of offending. Of course, a single paper does not produce the changes that have occurred since that time in a broad spectrum of crime policies and jurisdictions. Most likely the paper was catapulted into prominence because it was what many in government circles had been thinking for some time. More specifically it was consistent with mentalities of government that were beginning to shift away from a welfare state orientation. An ascendant neo-liberal politics was unevenly emerging across 'the West'. In this framework, as is now standard knowledge, welfare was regarded as counterproductive – creating dependency among its recipients, and discouraging self-reliance and individual enterprise and responsibility. In addition, this shift in the thinking of many governments brought forward a much greater stress on economic rationality, and in particular the idea that markets provided a model not simply for the economy but also for good government generally. This brought about a much more critical examination of crime control through welfare techniques.

Nothing in this development necessitated the rise of risk from the relatively obscure place it had occupied throughout the twentieth century. A series of features of neo-liberal governance were responsible for bringing it to the forefront. In summary form, these included the promise of risk as a preventative technology, especially as demonstrated in the health sector at the time. This risk-as-prevention approach was especially attractive to neo-liberal governance because it tallied so well with the emphasis on cost-effective governance. In business thinking, loss prevention was far preferable to the process of punishing, let alone the expensive process of correcting.

Risk-based models were also amenable to economic modelling. Based on prediction, their effects could be measured with respect to set goals and set timelines, in terms of the costs expended versus the losses avoided. For example, situational crime prevention interventions such as changing street lighting could be tailored to produce measurable local crime reduction effects in very short periods of time. Of course, risk could take other forms. The social welfare interventions such as social work with 'dysfunctional families' could be seen as reducing crime risks, but this way of reframing welfare was not applied at the time. One reason probably was the generally jaundiced attitude toward the helping professions. But in any case, such programs usually required long time-lines in order to register their effects, and they were also subject to all manner of disputes between diverse professional approaches. Cutting through the complex disputes by using a simple market technique like cost-benefit analysis made sense to economically minded governments in the era of 'nothing works'.

Much the same pattern of thought was to be applied to the penal domain. If criminals cannot demonstrably be corrected with any certainty, then at least risks could be reduced by incapacitating offenders in prisons. Moreover, prisons stripped of all the questionably effective welfare workers and probation officers would become much cheaper to operate. Besides, therapeutic interventions were subject to the criticism that they diminished offenders' responsibility for their actions by finding 'excuses' in poor education, disadvantaged upbringing, and so on.

A more positive 'what works' response emerged from among corrections researchers and advocates during the 1980s. This research-based development led to the adaptation of techniques originating in the welfare era to make them better fit cost-effective risk models. While often embracing interventions related to welfare variables, such as psychological or socioeconomic problems, they were more rigorously evaluated with respect to the reduction of crime risks. The result, to be explored in this chapter, included such approaches as 'risk-needs-responsivity'.

In such ways, a diverse array of risk-as-prevention programs became a widespread technology of crime control in a post-welfare state era. They ranged widely in form from prison incapacitation to the provision of psychological services, but shared in common a compatibility with a new hard-nosed mentality of government. Of course, the process whereby risk moved centre stage was not this simple, and it affected more areas than corrections and the built environment – most notably, policing, public education and sentencing. It is therefore to a more detailed analysis of such matters that the chapter now turns.

Policing risk

Crime prevention was not new to policing in the 1970s. Indeed, the foundations of the British police in the early nineteenth century were very clearly based on the assumption, explicated by Colquhoun, that 'the prevention of crimes and misdemeanours is the true essence of Police' (Colquhoun 1796: 259). Robert Peel, like Colquhoun, was part of the growth of preventative thinking that was more broadly associated with the development of liberal government in such fields as public health, hygiene and urban planning. With respect to police, Peel argued that 'the principal object to be attained is the prevention of crime. To this end every effort of the police is to be directed' (quoted by Gilling 1997: 108). Two approaches to prevention were developed from this beginning. The first was a loosely risk-based direction in which police were to be provided with information by the public, and would maintain surveillance on known offenders. It was intended to produce what would now be called 'intelligence-led' preventative policing.

However, this model fell by the wayside quite quickly. Partly this was because the governments of the time were also mindful of expense, yet it was difficult to demonstrate how many crimes had been prevented by police work. Much more demonstrable were the outcomes of a second 'preventative' approach in which police apprehended criminals through detective work and hot pursuit. The certainty of capture, it was assumed, would deter offenders and thus act preventatively. Furthermore, this second model of preventative policing fitted much better with the ethos of Victorian manhood in which police appear as crime 'fighters'. This was then, as now, much more attractive to police themselves (O'Malley and Hutchinson 2007). Henceforward, state policing marginalized crime prevention in the sense of intelligence-led policing – while both an organizational rationality and a police working culture embraced crime fighting (Hudson 1974: 293). Crime prevention took a back seat to crime fighting, and crime prevention increasingly became a duty assigned to a single crime prevention officer in each force, who gathered and circulated information about property crime patterns and preventative measures.

Little change occurred in this pattern until the 1960s. Around this time insurance companies responded to rising levels of theft and burglary against industry by pressuring governments to increase emphasis on crime prevention. Insurers demanded more government resourcing of advice to industry about situational crime prevention (for example, concerning improved lighting or deploying security guards), and also sought a shift in police participation toward community crime prevention. Police resisted such moves, arguing that every officer was also a crime prevention officer because the best way to prevent crime was to catch criminals: crime fighting remained their preferred approach. But pressure mounted into the 1970s as crimes against domestic property became a significant cost to insurers – a problem largely generated by the massive growth in portable valuables (especially radios, televisions, jewellery, cameras, etc.) in the burgeoning consumer society.

In the face of continued police resistance, one innovation by the insurance industry was to use insurance policies as a way of enforcing domestic security. Especially if they were burgled, policy holders were now required to report theft to police and to install security hardware as a condition of insurers continuing to provide coverage (O'Malley 1991). 'Community crime prevention' began with such humble origins, but around the same time, the arrival of neo-liberal governments began to increase pressure on police to develop a more business-like preventative stance. Despite continued police resistance, state policies mandated their involvement in new community crime prevention initiatives, some of which also had significant insurance industry involvement.

One of the most prominent developments was Neighbourhood Watch – often funded by insurance companies – in which police had the leading role. Basically these revived the preventative model advocated by Peel in which 'the community' was to advise police of suspicious individuals or risky situations. In addition, police were to advise the locals about the state of crime in their area, and provide information on how to reduce exposure to crime risks. In this way local and professional knowledge were to be brought together to reduce crime risks, and effective crime prevention would be the reward for communities that became 'active' on their own behalf. Perforce, police officers dedicated to crime prevention appeared in increasing numbers. It was a model that bore the hallmarks of neo-liberalism, making individuals more responsible for reducing their own risks, empowered by police advice and information, while making police more responsive to their 'customers' (O'Malley and Palmer 1996). This was of hotly debated efficacy, for it was argued that it merely deflected criminal activity to other, less well protected, targets. Nevertheless, this model proliferated into a large number of similar forms – such as 'Rural Watch', 'Small Business Watch' and 'Police Community Consultation Committees' – and was further linked to interventions by other state agencies (including the probation services) that manage crime risks 'in the community'.

At a broader level, state-based initiatives across Europe, North America and Australasia, such as the 'Safer Cities' movement of the 1980s, developed these models by linking them to public 'information' campaigns. Routinely these took the form of providing advice and data on crime risks. Again, major emphasis was placed on members of the 'community' – the actual and potential victims of crime – managing their own security. The British Home Office, for example, provided considerable information on how to avoid high risk crime situations. Their programs conformed to the growing assumption that policy should be 'intelligence led'. However, these often illustrated the ways in which risk appears to be an objective technique yet embodies political and value assumptions. In one of the more notorious examples, women were advised to avoid being out in public after dark, especially on their own. While this was based on copious statistical data indicating the risks to women's safety, it suffered a common failing of almost all official definitions of risk. The crime risks were identified by processing statistics of reported crime victimization and then projecting patterns and correlations into the future. Yet official statistics are often flawed, with serious consequences for risk policies.

As was pointed out in a very public campaign at the time, statistics on the crime victimization of women were riddled with gendered assumptions. To begin with, concerns were raised that by making women responsible for avoiding crime victimization on the streets the program was effectively blaming the victims, while at the same time relieving the state of responsibility for making the streets safe. But also, the 'stranger danger' assumptions of this policy were problematic. As feminist scholars argued (for example, Stanko 1996), violence inflicted by spouses and male friends and relatives almost certainly is a much greater risk than stranger danger, both in terms of likelihood and the severity and longevity of consequences. Yet statistics on domestic violence were hardly gathered at the time, and even now are universally recognized as vastly understating its prevalence because of disincentives to report offences to police. Women who reported domestic violence could suffer further violence from an angered spouse, could lose the financial support of the breadwinner, and could expect difficulties with the welfare of their children. As a result, not only were the risks to women under-estimated – with the concomitant claim that women were 'irrationally' afraid of crime – but also a large array of crime risks went unaddressed.

A related problem is that crime risk data may create vicious circles. Crime statistics reflect past police and court assumptions and practices, as well as actual offending patterns. Consequently, it is quite possible that the rules of thumb developed by police, often shared by community stereotypes, heighten the chances of racially and ethnically distinct youth being disproportionately targeted as suspects. To the degree this results in a disproportionate rate of convictions, the originating assumptions are seemingly confirmed by hard data. In turn, when these seemingly validated data are transformed into risk profiles, they translate into further police targeting and thus heighten still further the attention given to such minorities. Partly for such reasons, 'racial profiling' by police has been prohibited in Canada (O'Malley 2004).

If risks are 'gendered' and 'raced' in such fashion, class also can be built into risk modelling. Sometimes this begins from quite a low profile, for example, youth from working class suburbs may appear as out of place and threatening in middle class neighbourhoods or shopping centres; white youth appear as anomalies in black areas (Jefferson and Walker 1992). Such 'risky individuals' become the targets for public police attention, perhaps through Neighbourhood Watch information or because shopkeepers complain they scare off customers and are bad for business. But additionally they will tend to appear as the 'risky' targets for private police. Indeed, the phenomenal growth of private security over the past 40 years reflects a shift toward preventative policing in the employ of corporations and the middle class. Private security provides a 'customer oriented' form of policing simply because such police are *privately* employed: their key role tends to be prevention rather than capture and punishment. Businesses don't employ private security simply in order to replace public police, for whom concerns may be primarily with public order and moral issues. More specifically the concern is to provide a cost-effective form of property protection (Shearing and Stenning 1985). Insurers – whose interest is in risk and loss reduction – may require the deployment of private security on business premises for this very reason.

While it is not obvious that situational crime prevention represents a similar form of risk-based policing, I suggest that its function is precisely this, for it replaces a police presence – whether public or private in nature. Like coppers on the beat, or the 'silent policeman' of old – the dome placed in the road to keep traffic from cutting corners at intersections – it enforces the law by making offending more risky and less attractive. There is now a multitude of developments of this kind where statistical data have been gathered to identify 'criminogenic situations', and architectural solutions created to reduce their riskiness. Street lighting is improved, speed humps built, bushes removed in order to improve lines of sight, closed circuit television (CCTV) is installed to deter offending in elevators or corridors, and so on. While some of this is surveillance, much of it is simply behavioural channelling, sending offending behaviour elsewhere or making it difficult to perform at all. The fact that many CCTV monitors are either not connected to any recording apparatus (or are dummies, not connected to anything at all) is a clear example of these forms of deterrence. On the other hand, CCTV frequently provides prevention through other means. Constantly monitored television scanners can allow security guards to be literally panoptic, seeing around corners and to quite distant places, allowing instant despatch of security personnel where needed. Even where monitors are not manned, the recorded video information allows security and police later to identify both the modus operandi of offenders (triggering further situational crime prevention redesign) and in some cases the identity of the offenders themselves. Much situational crime prevention effectively is passive risk-policing based upon security information.

It is this informational characteristic of risk, the centrality of security information and its linking to prevention, that is also said to be transforming the work of public police. In their classic work on *Policing the Risk Society*, Ericson and Haggerty (1998) argue that the bulk of state police work is no longer detection and enforcement, but the gathering, creation and processing of security related information. Police have always been well placed to gather security data, but in the risk society, Ericson and Haggerty argue, this characteristic becomes definitive. Led by the insurance industry, many commercial, financial, educational, health and state welfare agencies demand security related information tailored to their needs. The result is argued to be that the police are governed by the 'risk knowledge formats' of such institutions. For instance, incident report sheets are structured in such ways that no matter what event police confront, it is recorded in pre-coded ways that make risk and security the focus. Another effect is that the risk focus has placed police forces in the centre of a new security-based configuration of governance that traverses all manner of contexts and issues. Thus the Canadian 'Shield of Confidence Home Security Program' involves the police, in conjunction with home-builders, insurance companies, and government building-code regulators, in a program that certifies the security technologies and design features of new homes. Builders are required to contact the police crime prevention branch on multiple occasions in the process of construction, and police are required to inspect and monitor the construction of the building (Ericson and Haggerty 1998: 157). Work of this kind brings a variety of diverse parties together in a risk network governed in new ways by police. In such ways policing is being transformed through the requirements imposed on them by the risk demands and frameworks of others.

While pointing to the impact of risk, Ericson and Haggerty may overstate the case, perhaps because of their adherence to Ulrich Beck's rather totalizing vision of the risk society. It is clear, for example, that pressures for security information are not the only forces impacting on police. Changes inspired by market-focused governments require strengthening of many traditional service and public order activities linked with audits of the public's satisfaction with 'their' police. Such demands by the public – as Campbell (2004) has found – may serve to reinforce many elements neutral or even hostile to risk regimes. For example, crime fighting may have been reined in from its dominance in the 1960s by new concerns with risk and prevention. However, many pressures keep crime fighting very prominent. Both police working culture and mass media representations ranging in focus from 'The Bill' to 'CSI' do much to preserve a primary place for the crime fighting model. Likewise, as Johnston (2000) has argued, the increased emphasis on risk and security ironically generates a level of insecurity among police 'customers'. This strengthens demands for visible reactive policing – as is indicated by the high profile police crazes for 'zero toler-ance', 'street sweeping' and other hard-line crime fighting strategies. As in the 1800s it may yet be that a convergence of recurring media and government demands for 'crackdowns' merge with public preferences for a visible police presence and rank and file police preferences to push policing in a crime fighting direction rather than further subordination to a risk society regime.

It is also important to recognize that the risk component of any policing program is rarely its only component. The danger with total-izing accounts of risk is that the mere presence of some element of risk calculation or of prevention results in an essentializing analytical manoeuvre that classifies a policing strategy as 'risk based'. Zero tol-erance policing (ZTP), for example, has certain elements that involve risk techniques, especially in terms of the deterrence of future offences. Clearly enough, however, to conflate all deterrence with risk would be to water down the latter concept and denude it of its historical specifi-city. Risk-based policing is characterized by the collection of informa-tion in order to make predictions, and the formation of preventative interventions based on these. It involves intervening before the event rather than reacting to it – even if the latter does have a preventative effect through deterrence. This was the difference between the two models of 'preventative' policing that Peel foreshadowed.

This should lead us to reject a binary way of thinking: that either something 'is' or 'is not' risk based. Rather it leads to a more complex vision in which the risk-based elements may or may not be those that are valorized in politics or practice at any one time. Thus while ZTP may be interpreted as containing risks within acceptable boundaries (Johnston 2000), its public, professional and political imagery was one much more consistent with reinforcing and restoring traditional crime fighting. In this sense, perhaps, ZTP illustrates the role of much more conservative political rationalities than are manifest in some other risk models. There is little of the laissez-faire approach to active policing implicit in much situational crime control, which, after all, is consistent with allowing for disorder as long as it does not cross certain risk boundaries. Such situational models of crime prevention embrace what David Garland (1996) refers to as a 'criminology of the self' – most clearly illustrated by classical criminology's centring of the rational choice offender. The offender, in short, could be any one of us presented with the right opportunity. Therefore, most situational crime prevention frameworks aim to eliminate situational opportunities rather than try to identify and target criminals. A degree of tolerance of social difference consistent with such approaches contrasts with such approaches as ZTP, in which social authoritarianism is much more prominent. In the latter, police and the public valorize a 'criminology of the other' – a vision focused on unacceptable individuals and actions that are to be punished and repressed in the name of a rigidly enforced set of standards identified as 'good order'.

In this way, risk appears as just one element in ZTP, not always or necessarily the most prominent, partly because conservative politics foregrounds moral agendas and preferred visions of hyper-conformity. The merely technical flavour of risk-minimizing, such as appears in policing rational choice offenders rather than folk devils and 'monsters', does not always sit well with this. Much the same is true for ostensibly preventative developments such as Megan's Laws in the US and Sarah's Laws in the UK. Such legislation established offender notification requirements that variously required violent and especially sex offenders to report to police periodically after serving their sentences. Some versions also required the offender's photograph and whereabouts to be posted on the internet, or sometimes to have identifying notices placed on their residences, specifying their offence record. The official justification for these measures is not that they are a form of further punishment, for the offender's sentence has been completed. Instead they are formally envisaged as a measure to prevent future offending by alerting the neighbours to the risks in their midst (Levi 2000). It is for this reason that these laws can be regarded as a form of risk-based policing.

Like community policing, such laws enlist 'the community' in its own defence, and they make offenders aware that they are under observation. If this reduces risks for the community (something never established with any certainty) it also increases risks for the ex-offenders. Together with their families they can be exposed to ostracism, at best, and vigilantism at worst. In the British case, the publication of such details by a tabloid newspaper led not only to the hounding of offenders but ultimately to the suicide of a wrongly identified man (Johnston 2000). In Jonathan Simon's (1998) analysis, the formal model of risk-based policing was better understood as a carrier for a 'politics of vengeance' than simply as an instance of the expansion of risk techniques. Hence, it may be necessary to think more subtly about the relationship between the presence of risk elements in a crime control technique, and about the reduction of that technique simply to one that is risk-focused. This point leads to a reconsideration of risk and the politics of policing.

While we can argue that the growth of risk-based crime prevention owes much to the development of neo-liberal politics, the latter are not the only politics at work in the current era. Clearly there are close alliances between neo-liberals and neo-conservatives – for example, with respect to the dislike of 'welfare' solutions to crime problems – but there are also important differences. In many respects neo-liberalism is relatively tolerant, preferring market-like and technical solutions to problems, whereas conservatives are more wedded to specifically moral agendas. We might say, for example, that neo-liberalism is much more comfortable with the morally neutral rational choice offender, the criminology of the self, and associated models of risk. On the other hand conservatives are more attached to discourses of stamping out and punishing moral evil rather than imagining offenders merely as Everyman presented with the right opportunity. This would be clear, for example, in different responses to programs governing illicit substance use that deploy such techniques as safe injecting facilities and decriminalizing possession in order to facilitate public health ends (O'Malley 2004). Where political conservatives are in the ascendancy, such 'technical' and seemingly morally neutral risk-oriented techniques – which in reality have their own moral agendas – may be wound back in favour of an emotive politics of vengeance.

Sometimes, this kind of political consideration is at least as important – and sometimes more important – than any common element of risk that various approaches embody. Forgetting this point in the hunt for evidence of risk's widening reach in the governance of crime is a profound danger to analysis. It can lead to a flattening of risk's diversity of form, function and meaning. If it is recognized that 'risk' is not a *neutral* technology, nor a *unified* technology of government, then the impact of politics becomes more clear. The form that risk techniques take appears to be shaped by such considerations as the nature of the dominant political ideology; by assumptions concerning race, class and gender; by the specific demands of institutions for the security of their operations, and so on. Different technologies and strategies of risk have quite distinct implications for how we govern and are governed. To the extent these points hold, then attention can be turned away from the kind of focus that risk-society theories highlight – risk's 'spread' – as if this were the only matter of concern. Instead more attention can be paid to the politics of risk: the struggles over what is to be identified as a risk, and who is to be targeted by risk techniques; over whether risk should merely incapacitate or should be invested with a responsibility for social reform; over who is to be given a say in deciding how risks should be responded to, and so on. In short, how risk is to be shaped.

The politics of risk and crime prevention

Perhaps it is time to illustrate the importance of differences in political stance and their impact on the nature of risk in a specific field of governance. Nowhere is the distinction between conservative and neoliberal governance through risk more clear than with respect to illicit drugs. The War on Drugs has been associated with a highly moralized zero-tolerance approach in which images of 'drug abusers' and 'drug addicts' exposes them to a kind of double whammy of control. The politics associated with 'Just Say No!' envisages those who take illicit drugs as making bad moral choices, of their own volition. As such they are exposed to the vicissitudes of a harsh penal regime, in which even possession of small amounts of mild drugs is met with long periods of imprisonment. Such 'drug abusers' have filled American prisons. However, once they become frequent consumers, they are imagined as trapped in a cycle of degradation, dependency and ultimately death. Such 'drug addicts' thus not only are to be imprisoned, but also subjected to compulsory medical interventions. Having 'lost' their free will and rationality, they must no longer be left to make their own choices. This imagery is a prime example of the criminology of the other – illicit drug users no longer appear as 'like us', and can be imagined as enemies of the good; the targets of a moral war.

Risk has been extensively mobilized as a weapon in this moralized struggle. Probably the most salient example has been the use of drug-testing technologies with respect to workplace drug testing. These have borrowed risk-assessment techniques from such success stories as random breath testing in traffic policing (O'Malley and Mugford 1992). As an objective scientific test, often under the justification of risks to workplace safety, they allow the procedures to appear neutral, directed at a risk rather than at specific individuals. In the name of risk and security, and administered by employers, they penetrate the private spaces into which the state is not normally imagined as 'intruding'. Workers may be randomly selected and subjected to invasive analysis; those who 'fail' these tests are excluded even where, for example, the drug concerned may have no demonstrable effect on the ability to perform work tasks effectively or safely. The same model is widely used in schools, and of course in sports – where, again, recreational drugs that have no performance-enhancing effects routinely lead to exclusions. Like ZTP, this technology is intended to have a double function: to draw and police a line between those who immorally create risks (or, very frequently, those who are assumed to be risk-creators even where evidence of risks is not supplied) and those who are imagined as the good and the harmless.

Again, it may be asked whether the more significant aspect of this technology is its risk component or the politics and morality of the program in which it is embedded. This becomes clear when programs of drug harm minimization are considered, such as have been mobilized in Australasia, Britain and Scandinavia (O'Malley 2004). A contrast between neo-liberal and neo-conservative politics, already mentioned, is that the former is much happier to leave things to the market. In the arena of drug politics this pitted the free marketeer Milton Friedman against the War on Drugs. In his view, if drugs were legalized and left to market forces, many harmful aspects of the drug problem would almost certainly diminish. For example, black markets are understood to increase prices. As prices drop with the demise of a black market, consequent upon legislation, pressures on users to commit crimes to pay for their habit would lessen. Corruption and violence would shrink as legitimate and competitive market practices predominate. Many of the health issues associated with illicit drug use would also decline as the grounds for unsafe practices, such as shooting-up in back alleys and drug adulteration, were eroded.

While usually stopping short of complete legalization, in many ways drug harm minimization programs of the 1980s and 1990s represented a kind of risk-based implementation of this economic vision. The basic premise of such programs was that all drug problems should be cast as risks: risks to health, to the economy, to careers, to quality of life and so on. The aim was to reduce – rather than unrealistically aiming to eliminate – these risks. One of the basic building blocks was the neo-liberal and economistic vision of all drug users as rational choice makers. This 'criminology of the self' was also promoted by arguing that licit pharmaceuticals, alcohol and tobacco were also problems to be governed by harm minimization, and were in many ways more harmful in population terms than illicit drugs.

The language and image of drug addiction and drug abuse were largely banished, for three related reasons. First, these were seen as demonizing users and socially isolating them, making them inaccessible to treatment. Second, demonizing also drove users underground and made it more likely that they would resort to unsafe drug administration, such as using dirty needles. Third, and probably most significant, it meant that as their rationality was not assumed to be impaired by drug dependence, they could be enlisted in the program of risk reduction. Coercion was therefore also to be minimized, and the stress was on making 'responsible choice makers' out of drug consumers. Risks, it was argued, were reduced when users and potential users made 'informed choices'. So a key part of the programs was to provide accurate information on the risks of drug use, especially of poly drug consumption, and even more so of unsafe drug administration (sharing needles, etc.). The risk-reducing benefits of seeking clinical care were pushed, including enrolment in methadone programs. In this latter instance, again, information was provided about the relative risks and costs of methadone usage, in the name of providing the basis for informed choices. Further risk reduction was to be achieved through establishing needle and syringe exchange programs, and providing safe injecting facilities.

Such programs clearly promoted a public health model. But this was not a model akin to the welfare state – which had by this time been widely discredited by the neo-liberal revolution. In its own imagery, it sought to 'empower' and responsibilize users rather than to make them dependent on experts. Expertise was to be 'on tap' rather than 'on top', at least in theory, to provide medical services and advice on request. In this way the model has much in common with community crime prevention, except that here criminal justice was not seen as a necessary aspect of the risk-reduction program. Rather, it was recognized that some aspects of crime control could be antithetical to harm minimization, for example, where it fostered demonization. Such imperatives led to instructions to police to turn a blind eye to drug use, which did not sit well with many, particularly police themselves. On the other hand, criminal justice was to be enlisted as a resource. It could be strengthened and given moral force, for example, in relation to those regarded as the primary risk creators, the drug traffickers.

It is at this point that harm minimization programs tend to cast off the mantle of scientific objectivity, and reveal the liberal utilitarian morality – the greatest good for the greatest number – that lurks just beneath the surface. Those who create significant risks for others in pursuit of their self-interested gain are, if necessary, to be incapacitated and punished.

While punishment of traffickers sits well with conservatives, the more tolerant elements of harm minimization programs are rarely accepted by them. Justified because they are judged by experts to reduce risk, and thus contribute to the public good, they do not attract support from those who regard drugs as a moral problem. To these people, risk reduction appears too technical, too neutral, too tolerant. But perhaps this 'technical' character of harm minimization reveals how such programs may have other dangers lurking within them. The tolerance afforded to those who embrace responsible drug use is always conditional on its demonstrated effectiveness in risk minimization. Because the definition of risks and of which risks are to be acted upon resides with expertise, this delivers considerable political and governmental power into their hands.

The point of this brief excursion into drug harm minimization is not only to emphasize the importance of attending to risk's diversity and to draw attention to the ways in which it is shaped and mobilized differently by diverse political and moral agendas. It is also to make clear that like other forms of governance, risk therefore is a field of political conflict, and is therefore open to change. Risk is not simply a fixed and narrow technology that we must either accept or reject. We can change its form and function quite dramatically. Unfortunately, this is not the sense that emerges from the largely pessimistic literature on what David Garland (2001) influentially has named and described as 'the culture of control'.

Risk and the culture of control

In Garland's account, risk takes its place as part of a movement that has eroded or subordinated welfare corrections since the 1970s. Garland argues that this movement arises from complex causes: the failure of penal modernism to bring down robustly high crime rates; the associated exposure of the professional middle classes to crime, and the consequent diminution of their support for correctional justice; the rise of neo-liberal government with its hostility to welfare; and the rise of risk as a technique for managing social problems. The resultant has been a governing telos that has sought to govern crime through control of criminal behaviour rather than by attending to the welfare and reform of offenders. Risk, for example in the models of situational crime prevention and Megan's Laws, took its place in this assemblage, focusing on the containment and incapacitation of offenders. As will be seen shortly, this same characterization was true for risk-based incapacitation in prisons.

What I argue, is not that Garland is wrong in his account, although I will shortly argue that his account under-estimates the extent and importance of exceptions (Hutchinson 2006). Rather, the point is that negative, crime control, risk models are only some of the possible models of risk. They are the ones mobilized by a crime control philosophy that has shaped all manner of other techniques and sanctions to serve the ends of control – principally containment, incapacitation and exclusion. By implication, I would suggest against Garland that 'risk' should not be regarded as a formative element of the culture of control. The key formative element is the crime control ethos which gives to risk techniques' specific forms and functions, and which have been sketched out in this chapter. Nevertheless, Garland overlooks the extent to which risk techniques, such as drug harm minimization, which attend to the welfare of drug users and to their reintegration rather than their social exclusion, can thrive in such an environment, and can be consistent with 'neo-liberal' politics. Likewise, accounts of the culture of control overlook the extent to which such programs can be seen as a form of resistance in the face of more conservative demands. They may even be regarded as possible bases from which a critical criminology may build alternative practices and politics of risk. More broadly, it implies that instead of the constant mapping of the ways of domination, of the inexorable march of the culture of control, the focus might be shifted more in the direction of a criminology of possibilities, rather than a pessimistic vision that seems to offer little progressive hope.

This more hopeful interpretation may lead us to reconsider some of the forms of risk-based techniques developed in the period since 'what works?' displaced the gloomier motto of 'nothing works', for example, developmental crime prevention. In a nutshell, developmental crime prevention has sought to identify and deal with crime risks as they appear early in the development of what were once called 'pre-delinquents' but now are more often referred to as 'at risk young people'. This shift in terminology could be seen as indicative of the change from a welfare approach to a culture of control. No doubt this is partly true. Thus, with respect to the 'crime risk factor' of child abuse, it is stressed that '(t)he professional focus on the medical model popularised in the 60s' has changed. Now, 'the notion of community and neighbourhood services to *assist* vulnerable families with child rearing in order to diminish abuse is gathering momentum ... The thrust of our work has been maximising the empowerment of families' (Tolley and Tregeagle 1998: 6–8). Certainly this is very neo-liberal talk. But perhaps a better description of the situation in many jurisdictions is that social work and related professions are not so much being dismantled (as implied in Rose's (1996) image of 'the death of the social') as translated into forms and practices more consistent with the assumptions of economic and individual responsibility that characterized the new politics.

For example, in an influential Australian program of the late 1990s, the 'empowering' practices of developmental crime prevention bear a very strong resemblance to the interventions of the welfare era – involving 'family support, early intervention, and home visiting programs' (NCP 1999: 17). Likewise, developmental psychology's list of crime-risk factors – 'family isolation', 'inadequate parenting', 'single parents', 'attachment difficulties', 'low self-esteem', 'poor social skills', 'poor cognitive skills' and so on, is seemingly identical with the lists of causes of crime with which it worked under the welfare state. The preventative and rehabilitative agendas of the former era are thus reintroduced even though regarded as a 'new' approach to crime prevention (for example, Homel 1998). Similarly, Canadian approaches of the same period recommend that a comprehensive crime prevention strategy provide 'educational, social and health services', and urge that it 'is essential that this strategy address child poverty' (CPCC 1997: 11). The Australian National Crime Prevention (NCP 1999: 13) lists 'socio-economic disadvantage', 'population density and housing conditions', 'lack of support services' and 'social or cultural discrimination' among its crime-related 'cultural and community factors'. The agenda, although situated within a risk discourse, gives expression to the welfare-social rationalities, and in so doing begins to hint at social justice and kinds of socially – rather than individually – ameliorative programs that were associated with the welfare state (Stenson and Watt 1999).

Now, as Garland (2001) among others has stressed, this does not represent a carte blanche for the social professions to return to business as usual. Emphasis on cost benefit analysis operates as a 'firewall', and benefits are not to be measured in to old ways. Such programs are to be focused on results measured in terms of crime prevention. These are, in other words, not 'welfare' but 'crime control' programs subject to strict evaluation, a technique that – because it demands measurable results in a relatively short time-span – restricts the scope of 'socially' oriented projects of the older variety. It is essential to pay attention to this new regime. But too little attention is paid to the unanticipated consequences of allowing welfare categories and mentalities back into the fold. In the 1990s proposals began to emerge that advocated the formation of long-term and large-scale programs addressing social conditions, by proposing that each step can be evaluated as part of a long-term chain. Others emphasize that as developmental programs deal with children from birth (or before), then the term of evaluation has to cover a minimum period of ten years, and frequently longer (for example, Everingham 1998, Rand Corporation 1998). Long-term, large-scale and long-range projects reappeared. Equally important is the fact that evaluations – which in practice proved neither cost benefit nor even quantitative in form – were often carried out by bearers of the same knowledges. For example, the Rand Corporation (1998), based on data generated by the US Accounting Office – the maw of the neo-liberal beast – argued that it is 20 times more cost-effective to provide early intervention to every family than to pay for the costs of child abuse, low birth weight babies and the crime risks that are traced from these sources.

As critical criminologists themselves should recognize, professional training and development are multivocal. Especially where university education is a component, there are always likely to be forms of knowledge and practice, aims and sympathies that do not simply conform to the narrow mentalities of crime control. With respect to crime prevention, as I have suggested also with respect to police, the terrain of risk is a good deal less stable than would be supposed by some of the more pessimistic and totalizing readings. Rather than imagining risk as 'hegemonic' or as capable of only one reading, we need to take more seriously the idea that risk itself is a domain of struggle and also that its implications are not fixed or always foreseeable. By the same token, I am not naively putting forward a vision of heroic and eventually successful resistance. Resistance takes many forms, its success is neither guaranteed nor its outcomes knowable in advance. As well, it may be that the unintended consequences of developments in policy and practice play a major role in transforming or curtailing risk of the 'control' sort. For the moment, at least, I simply want to urge the need to pay attention to potential and existing sources of change, rather than automatically adopting a demoralizing focus only on the inevitability of risk as a key technology of an exclusionary polity.

Risk and the 'new penology'

In the early 1990s, one of the most influential examinations of the rise of risk-based crime control proposed that a 'new penology' was emerging in which actuarial calculation was pivotal (Feeley and Simon 1992, 1994). In the prevailing approach to justice under penal modernism, the individual case was paramount. Sentencing decisions were largely based on the diagnoses and prognoses provided by experts in the probation and parole services. Sentencing reports examined the specific individual, his or her social background as well as criminal record, and recommended a sentence based on these data. In turn, the sentencing official took these into account (and in countries such as Australia and Britain usually conformed closely to their recommendations) together with the details of the offence at hand. Sentences were to be proportional in some degree both to the need of the offender for correction and to the gravity of the offence. However, Feeley and Simon detected a new pattern emerging in which both of these principles were being undermined.

Justice was no longer to be offender focused. Instead it was increasingly to be focused on the needs of the community for protection. Sentencing was to be based on tariffs graduated according to the risks posed by the offender, as indicated by present and preceding offence record. The details of the individual case were relevant only insofar as they assigned the offender to a risk category for which an appropriate sentence was prescribed. In turn, the length of sentence was no longer understood to be dictated by the seriousness of the crime or the correctional needs of the offender as assessed by judges and experts. Rather, the length of the sentence was to be proportional to the magnitude of the risk, the intent being to remove significant risks from the community.

In line with this, the prison regime was no longer primarily to be correctional. In the new penology, the penal regime would reduce risks, and thus prisons were to be places of incapacitation. Security completely displaced correction as the institutional goal. A new managerial ethos developed around this shift. Emphasis was no longer on complex and disputed questions about declines in recidivism or about successfully reformed offenders. Instead, stress was placed on throughputs, especially the numbers of offenders processed by the system. The ambiguities of whether prisoners were reformed were to be displaced by the calculable precision of risk reduction. Given that offenders create risks, and given that prisons incapacitate, then the sheer number of offenders incarcerated multiplied by the length of their incarceration, indicated a certain volume of risk reduction. If the removal of correctional regimes in prisons reduced the costs per capita, so much the better. Even evidence of high rates of recidivism after release – once the bane of reform regimes – now became evidence that the right people had been incarcerated and underlined the value of locking risks away for a long time.

As part of this development, all manner of incapacitating innovations began to appear under the banner of risk reduction 'in the community'. Megan's and Sarah's Laws represent one variation on this theme. Many others appeared more distant from a politics of vengeance. House arrest reduced the state costs of imprisonment enormously. It could be strengthened by requiring 'inmates' to report by telephone at regular intervals – or to answer computer-generated phone calls. Electronic anklets or bracelets were woven into this fabric. They were also applied in other incapacitating regimes where offenders were prohibited from moving into certain social spaces – near schoolyards, near their former partner's home, and so on. Curfews emerged as a favourite technique, especially for managing troublesome youth, turning parents into contractually bound gaolers. Even probation was widely adapted to this kind of end, requiring the offender to report frequently, but in practice offering little else than verification of a presence. Nothing in this was correctional. In such ways, risk-incapacitation was seen to leak out of the prisons – in much the same fashion that a previous generation of criminologists had identified community corrections as the prison-break of discipline, creating 'the punitive city' (Cohen 1979).

While many criminologists took literally the vision of this risk-incapacitating regime as the future of penology, the authors themselves

(Simon and Feeley 1995) quickly corrected their predictions. They recognized that risk-based sentences were attractive at a time when welfare corrections were regarded as failures, when protection for the public was high on the agenda, and when fixed tariff based sentences were seen as better than the apparent inconsistencies of individualized justice. It was also widely recognized that actuarial assessments provided better predictors and judicial or expert judgement, and were even more 'just' because they were not open to the biases of the court (Glaser 1985). Despite this, Simon and Feeley suggested that there were significant sources of resistance to 'actuarial justice'.

In the American context, where judges frequently are elected, such a 'technical' regime as risk was seen not to give room for the expression of community outrage and of moral condemnation. Even though sentences were frequently severe, the spirit of the times – described by Pratt (2006) as 'penal populism' – demanded just desserts and retribution. Judges themselves also were a source of resistance to risk-based sentencing. As Freiberg (2000) has argued, judges resisted the importation of risk-based tariffs because they offended both the judiciary's sense of what justice is, and of how they viewed their role in delivering it. Moreover, judges had many means at hand to thwart the new regime, most obviously because offences and offenders' records could be redefined so that they did not fall into the categories governed by risk-based sentences. In the United States, plea bargaining also significantly interfered with risk-based sentencing, as charges were dropped or reduced so that the risk-based sentences would not apply. Significant problems were created for prison officials as a result of the increasing number of prisoners coming into already overcrowded institutions, and support for sentencing mitigation was passed back up the line (Austin et al. 1999).

The result has been the emergence of a very uneven patchwork of risk-based sentencing. With respect to certain high profile offences – especially violent and sexual assault offending – risk rationales have become prominent. Sentences are shaped and justified by reference to shifting the burden of risk onto offenders and away from potential victims. In other examples, such as 'three strikes and you're out' legislation, the place of risk has become secondary to that of other social agendas. Indeed, it is debateable whether risk was ever a critical issue with respect to 'three strikes'. Certainly some evidence was put forward that once an offender had been convicted of three indictable offences then the likelihood of re-offending was extremely high. But it was the baseball imagery and the claims that such offenders had forfeited the right to be members of a decent society that were publicly mobilized (Greenberg 2002). In several jurisdictions, such approaches to sentencing were vilified as racist. In the Northern Territory of Australia, for example, a high profile campaign pointed out that because a large number of Aboriginal people already were 'high risks' in such a schema, and because Aboriginal people had high rates of conviction in court, then the impact of such laws could only be to increase their already disproportionate over-representation in prisons. A nationally prominent Royal Commission had only recently made clear that numbers of Aboriginal deaths in custody were unacceptably high. Subsequent policy interventions had been directed at reducing both Aboriginal over-representation and the numbers of deaths in custody. In this environment, whatever arguments there were about risk reduction, they were overwhelmed by a politics of quite a different colour to that associated with 'three strikes'. The legislation was thrown out after the next election (O'Malley 2003).

Again, the significance of politics and of resistance to certain forms of risk-based policy and practice comes to the fore. The 'new penology' did not emerge as predicted. Not only was it to be unevenly installed, but even where risk did have a very substantial impact on what goes on in prison, things could look very different to incapacitation. As with crime prevention there are different ways of mobilizing risk. It is possible to agree that many prisons were merely risk-incapacitating warehouses – although of course many had always been warehouses. Yet a major way in which risk has had an impact in prison has been to reform and redirect correctional 'welfare' sanctions rather than to remove them.

Technologies of risk in the prison

A key argument in favour of actuarial rather than expert and judicial decision-making in justice was its superior predictive power. Justice officials could not match the accuracy of predictions based on the processing of vast amounts of data into correlation matrices. This was not a new development in the 1980s, the best-known precursor being the work of Glueck and Glueck (1946) who developed a variety of predictive instruments based on statistical data relating to offenders and their official and self-reported rates of recidivism. While they sought to have these techniques taken up by judges and parole boards, their efforts were largely unsuccessful. Prior to this, a number of prominent US criminologists had developed similar predictive scales. But only one – Burgess (1928, 1936) – had achieved even limited success when the state of Illinois appointed sociologist-actuaries to develop improved actuarial tables (Ohlin 1951, Glaser 1962). In Britain, Mannheim and Wilkins (1955) developed parallel techniques and used them to achieve significantly better predictions than the judgements of prison experts. Riding on the back of such work, Wilkins, working with Gottfredson, was commissioned by the US Board of Parole to develop statistically driven predictors of parole outcomes, which formed the basis of the federal parole guidelines and were adopted by a majority of state parole boards (Glaser 1985).

Such early developments received surprisingly little attention from critical criminologists perhaps because risk remained embedded in the broader framework of 'welfare' correctional justice. Feeley and Simon (1992), for example, argue that such uses of risk were deployed to improve reform, through identifying problems to be addressed, such as alcoholism or unemployment. Critical attention was drawn to actuarial predictions in relation to probation and parole primarily when, after the 1980s, they were seen to be part of a much wider deployment of risk in the context of the developing culture of control. In this setting, risk techniques were increasingly used to determine whether or not prisoners represented too much of a risk to the community to be eligible for release.

As initially envisioned, risk tools would displace biased and unreliable predictions made by those wielding professional judgement. However, this is not how things have panned out. As with the judiciary, probation and parole officers have resisted the displacement or subordination of their professional expertise by risk instruments that effectively reduced them to mere ciphers administering a questionnaire. On the one hand, this resulted in covert actions that undermined the risk instruments. For example, in Britain probation officers admitted assessing offenders according to their professional judgement, and then completing the risk schedule in order to produce a score that corresponded to this (Kemshall 1998). Such resistance is important to recognize. However, it does little to affect the institutional dominance of risk, and is always available to frustration through further refinements in administrative techniques.

More significant, as Kemshall (2003: 67) records, have been challenges to risk instruments per se. Thus the National Association of Probation Officers rejected the Offender Group Reconviction Score both because it displaced professional judgement and because it was a flawed instrument that was in practice a poor predictor. In this process, questions of individual justice and risk came to the fore because, it was argued, risk scores related to statistical distributions: they do not apply to particular individuals for whom the probability of re-offending is unknown. If professional judgement alone can attend fully to the individual case, the implication – in the face of opposition from risk advocates – was claimed to be that risk scores are no more than an aid, a position that was ultimately accepted by the Home Office (Kemshall 2003: 66–8).

Again, such 'victories' are not the end of a fairy story in which 'good' professional expertise triumphs and 'bad' risk is deposed. This was merely one more development in an ongoing political struggle. It should be recognized, for example, that wherever risk is placed in such decision-making schemata, it is still set within a context where the focus of parole has shifted markedly away from the offender's needs and toward the risks created by the offender. Even so, this confirms that risk techniques take their form and function from the broader – and always contested – governing environment that puts them to work. The resulting configuration of risk is often profoundly ambiguous in political terms, and may be part of a 'late modern rehabilitation'; a revival of penal modernism (Robinson 2008). Perhaps nowhere is this clearer than with respect to the delivery of welfare and therapeutic services in the prison.

Feeley and Simon's initial vision of actuarial justice was that it promoted penal incapacitation as risk-reduction. Yet even as they wrote, the more optimistic 'what works?' counter-reaction led to alternative uses of risk being developed. These blossomed into what was later referred to as 'risk-needs' analysis or 'risk-needs-responsivity'. The key idea was that therapeutic sanctions had been wasteful not because they were therapeutic, but simply because they had aimed at meeting prisoner needs and had not been tightly linked to crime reduction. The invention of the concept of 'criminogenic needs' sought to unite prisoner needs and crime reduction. It gave rise to the use of risk-based techniques to identify those treatment services that would benefit the prisoner *and* demonstrably reduce an offender's risk of future criminal behaviour (Andrews and Bonta 2006).

From the point of view of its advocates (largely psychologists), and even in a qualified way some critical criminologists (Ward and Maruna 2007), this approach restored the offender to a position of centrality. It was also understood to re-inject the welfare-rehabilitation orientation and expert intervention back into the prison. Such 'risk-needs-responsivity' approaches became extensively used in Canada, Australasia, Europe, the USA, Britain and elsewhere (Ward and Maruna 2007). Also, it is now becoming clear that their officially registered success has been responsible for the re-introduction of revised pre-sentence reports that use risk-needs assessment tools to determine whether offenders merit imprisonment (Bloomenfeld 2007).

Politically speaking, this can be seen as a further example of the resistance of the social, similar to that already seen with respect to drug harm minimization and developmental crime prevention. Certainly, set against the bleak imaginary of the 'new penology' that did little more than incapacitate, this claim surely holds some water, and provides a corrective to the rather bleaker forecasts of a 'new penology'. But from another point of view (Garland 2001) it represents a further instantiation of the culture of control, for rehabilitation is only countenanced as long as it serves the purpose of crime reduction. While Garland and others are quite correct to argue thus, it is not clear how far this is a problem. Re-establishing a rehabilitative regime in the penal domain is itself an advance of sorts. After all, much of the grief and anger expressed by critical criminologists over the 'punitive turn' has been linked precisely to their observation that the 'welfare sanction' and 'penal modernism' had been overthrown.

In his 2004 presidential address to the American Society of Criminology, Frank Cullen (2005) argued that a re-assertion of rehabilitation in the US was largely the effect of work by criminologists who 'used rigorous science' to show that popular punitivism was ineffective and that rehabilitation could work. Of course, it is still a matter of concern that risk may be mobilized in repressive regimes. It may also be doubted whether this is 'rigorous science', for such measures have been extensively challenged (Maurutto and Hannah-Moffat 2007). Even so, it is not altogether clear why its role in reasserting rehabilitation (with caveats to be explored shortly) cannot be regarded as politically positive. Not perfect, perhaps not even very good, but a step away from the abyss.

Certainly it is viewed as progressive by its principal developers such as Don Andrews and his co-workers (Andrews and Dowden 2007: 440–1). They claim that support should be given to a tool that promotes rehabilitation, demonstrates the futility of punishment in the absence of treatment, protects potential victims and promotes the 'ethical, legal, decent, humane, efficient, and just pursuit of reduced offending'. Yet there are many telling critiques of this specific mobilization of risk. Kelly Hannah-Moffat and her colleagues (Hannah-Moffat 1999, 2005, Maurutto and Hannah-Moffat 2007) have drawn attention to serious methodological and operational flaws in the use of such instruments. In particular they have pointed to the inappropriate use, in dealing with women inmates, of risk assessment instruments developed from data relating to male offenders. In their view, the data produce inappropriate responses, for example, to equate violence by women with the considerably more lethal and harmful violence by men works considerably to the detriment of women when prison security classification and parole decisions are at issue.

Likewise, Maurutto and Hannah-Moffat (2007) have argued that male-derived risk-needs analyses in women's prisons may often result in creating major harms for female inmates. For example, identifying family issues as not relevant to criminogenic risks and thus not to be dealt with by prison services may possibly be of little consequence for many men. However, it creates major emotional and other traumas for many women inmates. This is made worse by the fact that family issues may be criminogenic for women – data do not allow this to be discounted because the small number of women prisoners does not allow development of useful actuarial data needed for risk calculations. Nor is this the end of such problems. The identification of certain criminogenic needs as 'psychiatric' may be used to delay the release of women prisoners and to increase the level of security to which they are subjected – rather than working only (or at all) to assist with the life problems they confront. It has also been argued that pre-sentence reports built up around risk-assessment do not differentiate between types of recidivism – so that trivial and serious instances of reoffending are recorded the same way.

Risk and representation

Perhaps all these objections to risk-needs-responsivity could be dismissed as methodological issues readily corrected. It is difficult to believe that any prison regime could be developed without problems of this sort cropping up. It is the proper work of criminologists to identify such problems both in terms of producing risk reduction and, equally importantly, to defend the interests of the voiceless subjects of such regimes. But these critiques address problems in design and implementation. They do not attack the heart of risk technologies as such. If the concern is with promise or dangers of risk techniques per se, or with the place and implications of risk measures and tools in crime control, then other questions need to be asked.

Nevertheless, the analysis of risk-needs-responsivity (RNR) as a promising form of risk-based intervention does suggest some key issues that are central to risk as such. One of the most critical of these, as suggested already with respect to drug harm minimization, concerns who has the right to define what is a risk. Or more properly, the question might be posed as: what are the consequences of defining risks in different ways? Critics have suggested that 'criminogenic needs' is itself a highly problematic category. As noted above, these 'needs' may not coincide with other needs. The needs of mothers to be with their children, for example, may be excluded if not criminogenic. Likewise Maurutto and Hannah-Moffat (2007: 471) make the point that officially defined criminogenic needs differ from many socio-cultural definitions of needs and especially indigenous people's definitions of needs. Much the same point can be made with respect to the criticism that RNR and related techniques do not address more holistic welfare needs because of their focus on crime control. In one of the few sympathetic treatments of RNR carried out by critical criminologists, Ward and Maruna (2007: 80–5) have pushed this point further. They argue that because of its narrow focus on expert-defined criminogenic needs, RNR does not maximize its effectiveness even in its own terms. This is because 'clients need to "buy in" to a rehabilitation strategy, believe it is the best thing for them and actually want to succeed at it'. In other words, in order for the model to achieve the risk-reducing ends it sets itself, there has to be some convergence between officially defined criminogenic needs and the needs as defined by the offender.

Surely the key problem – and a problem clearly implied by Hannah-Moffat and others – is that risk is defined by expertise. But we have seen already that such definitions are not necessarily 'objective' merely because they are produced by scientifically rigorous techniques. Women, as the frequent targets of violent and sex crimes, have been seen to define risk in rather different ways to criminal justice experts. Women prisoners may prioritize the risks to the family that experts dismiss as irrelevant. Women in the community may seem to 'exaggerate' the risk of public assault beyond its statistical probability. But this may be because of its potential for sexual assault that escalates the magnitude of the perceived risk beyond what appears 'rational' to male experts. Indigenous offenders and communities may have yet other assessments of risk, relating to risks to their traditional practices and beliefs or to the risks that police represent to their young people. Drug users' views on the risks of assault by police may be ignored altogether even by the most assiduous public health program, while the objections of parents to having safe injecting facilities in their neighbourhoods, because they may create risks to their children's exposure to drug use, may be dismissed by experts as 'nimbyism'.

A simple answer to all these problems is that criminal law is determined by democratic politics, and thus provides the democratic solution to what a crime risk is. Yet this leaves many difficult questions unanswered. What of the politically sensitive issue of cultural differences in risk definitions? What if risk programs are destined to fail if they do not take account of variable definitions of risk? What if women's experiences and understandings of risk clash with those of a male-centred criminal justice system? What is the 'appropriate' way to deal with those people and actions defined as creating crime risks? What of those 'at risk' people who are subjected to intervention before they have offended or after they have been punished? What of the plight of all the so-called 'false positives' – the inescapable proportion of people who are wrongly predicted to be offenders yet suffer the consequences? How insignificant does a crime risk have to be for us to ignore it? These are questions that escape the kind of analysis that can be offered in a book such as this, and for the most part, that escape the criminological studies this book relies upon. In large measure this is because they are not theoretical questions or research questions. They are the *political* questions that research and theory cannot answer but cannot escape or resolve. They underlie each and every instance in which risk is applied to the governance of crime, just as much as to such health-risk issues as birth defects, or to issues of risks to the environment.

For the moment, the matter will be left to lie here to be reconsidered in the conclusions. Yet one of its implications is that if risk cannot be objective, neither is it necessarily politically conservative. If risks are defined by experts, they are not only defined by experts. In turn, it implies that all the developments analysed in this chapter have taken their character because, historically, they are part of the culture of control. Risk did not have to be like this, nor is it all that it can become. The fact that risk has attained such prominence thus makes all the more urgent and important the abandonment of the vision of risk as negative. Risk is not going to go away. Therefore the time is overdue to consider how risk can be shaped to work in other ways. Part of this reconsideration might lie in thinking about how risk is embraced precisely by those who are the criminal subjects of risk management.

THREE

crime, risk and excitement

Most crime has always involved some degree of conscious or unconscious risk-taking. Criminal behaviour is thus, in important ways, set at 180 degrees to contemporary crime control along an axis of risk. Much crime control aims to increase the risks confronting offenders and thus to deter crime. This may sound obvious, but it's not. To begin with, the idea of criminals as conscious risk-takers, as opposed to simply evil-doers, owes its modern origins to the classical criminology of Bentham and Beccaria. The idea of generating a systematic and continuously operating crime control apparatus intended to increase the risk to offenders is quite modern, and in the common law world this owes its origins to the capitalist and liberal 'revolutions' of the late eighteenth and early nineteenth century. Moreover, these revolutions were associated with a wide-ranging project to transform the bulk of the population into calculating risk-*avoiders*. Everyday life for much of the population became increasingly circumscribed by institutions based on a model that worked more or less continuously to stamp out unwarranted risk-taking – as defined by liberal utilitarian dogma of the time – among working people. In this way, risk-taking could appear as a form of resistance, for example, through upholding old ways of drinking, gambling and 'carnivalesque' entertainment. No doubt 'criminal' resistance of this sort rarely had a formally political component, but much of it represented a refusal to conform with a liberal utilitarian discipline imposed by the respectable middle classes.

Since its heyday in the late nineteenth century, the idea that crime as risk-taking is diametrically opposed to an accepted image of responsible subjects as risk-avoiders has been significantly, if unevenly, eroded. This is most obvious if we consider the late twentieth century neo-liberal preference for subjects to become more active risk-takers on their own behalf, for example, in speculating on the stock market, engaging in individual business enterprise, escaping 'dead end' jobs, and so on. The market, as a technique for taking risks in order to maximize opportunities and quality of life, came to be applicable to all.

This neo-liberal ideology may have been only the most explicit and recent flowering of change that had been underway since the turn of the twentieth century. I will argue that a governmental commitment to enforcing risk aversion as the expectation for most people, gradually eroded with the rise of a consumer economy. Slowly at first, the idea spread that working people could legitimately seek self-fulfilment through consumption rather than devote themselves to frugal self-denial. Novelty and excitement – worrisome pathologies even in the late 1800s – slowly became more acceptable as goals available to all. Indeed after the 1950s, excitement, in which risk-taking plays a prominent role, became a *valued* possibility for everyone. As risk-taking has become more acceptable, so some 'traditional' forms of crime – notably gambling – have been transformed into respectable activities, run by governmentally valued 'leisure industries'. More important, whereas once a reasonably clear line could be drawn between responsible risk avoiding behaviour and crimes and deviations that embraced risk, now that line has become more blurred. More 'risk-taking' crime can appear not as an affront to the very image of the responsible subject, nor even as a form of resistance to a dominant morality, but more frequently as a mirror image – a 'subterranean' expression – of mainstream values (Hall et al. 2008).

Ironically, then, as risk minimization has become an increasingly central approach of crime control, it confronts a popular culture and an economy in which certain kinds of risk-taking have become more acceptable. Perhaps this is not an irony. Ulrich Beck (1992) would suggest that both are expressions of the rise of the 'risk society' in which risk consciousness – thinking of issues in life in terms of their riskiness – has become dominant. I think we need not go down this track, some of the pitfalls of which have been mentioned earlier. Perhaps, as I suspect, this collision of governmental risk minimization and embracing risk is simply a contingency, of the sort history is littered with. More certainly it has been organized by neo-liberal governments into a framework where all subjects are responsible for their own risks, and should become competent in deciding which risks to embrace and which risks to minimize. One of the implications is that as risk-taking has become more salient and has become valued in new ways, so a politics of risk-taking becomes more pressing for criminologists to engage with. Such a politics should bring to the forefront competing, diverse, ambiguous definitions of what risks are worth taking (according to whom), and how 'embracing risk' should be valued and dealt with. In this chapter, I will explore in more detail the arguments about crime as risk-taking, leaving for the conclusions the question of what a politics of risk-taking and risk-minimizing could look like in the domain of crime and its governance.

Risk-taking and the world of classical liberalism

Bentham's rational choice offender not only weighed up the costs and benefits of any action, but also assessed their relative probabilities. For this reason, Bentham and other classical criminologists put great emphasis on increasing the certainty of capture, over and above the prevailing eighteenth century idea that deterrence would be achieved by fear of severe punishment. The 'rational' offender would effectively be deterred by a penalty only marginally in excess of the prospective gains, where capture was made highly likely. This contrast with the spectacular but sporadic regimes of punishment associated with the pre-liberal years was not only associated with the rise of the 'discipline' of docile bodies, as Foucault argues, but equally with a disciplinary vision of a form of subject who should take on what Bentham (1962 [1789]) called 'the yoke of foresight'. Everyone was expected look to the future in a calculative fashion. While, of course, this was not entirely new, what was novel was the expectation that *all* subjects should plan ahead, that this would be an expectation of virtually every facet of life *at all times*. Subjects would be made personally responsible for the foreseeable consequences – the productive and the harmful risks – of their actions. It was assumed that most people would benefit from this rationally calculative activity, as wealth would accumulate across the society. Yet the idea that most people would become capitalists was very far from the minds of those such as Bentham. Foresight in the lives of most people was expected to be directed more toward making provision against the harmful potentialities of a free market economy.

'Prudence' is the name most associated with this regime of risk-avoidance and harm minimization. Its twin components were both disciplinary: a discipline of diligent labour matched with a discipline of thrift and saving. This, it was expected, would create a certain kind of freedom – an 'independence' of individuals who would be financially autonomous and thus able to direct their lives without being a burden on others. It was a way of life that required constant self-denial and deferred gratification. For those who failed in this regime, the workhouse provided both a deterrent spectre and a harsh regime of training. For those who refused or rebelled against this regime, or who were constituted by courts in this fashion, the prison provided a similar but harsher alternative. Drunkenness, vagrancy, indigence, gambling, disorderly behaviour and idleness formed a pool of behaviours that consigned a vast number of offenders and their families to one or other of these forbidding institutions. They were offences against prudence, against the demand to look forward and prepare – to govern life's harmful risks 'responsibly'.

Naturally, for some subjects, there was an upside. Capitalists, speculators, explorers and military adventurers were risk-taking heroes of nineteenth-century society, but it was taken for granted that these roles were restricted by class, race and gender to a handful of people. For example, women were barred from stock markets, even had they the necessary access to money, because they were regarded as too irrational or too weak for this high risk domain (O'Malley 2004). Likewise, explorers were almost universally men (white men at that) who either had personal wealth to afford the risks, and/or who had the class contacts to provide necessary funding. Even for the entrepreneurs the spectre of prudence lurked in the background, for it was always assumed that their ventures would be within their means, and thus failure would not 'recklessly' threaten their independence. Over and above each of these required qualifications, such risk-taking was justified because it was also assumed that these activities were for the benefit of the many.

Capitalists took risks in order to produce wealth and jobs for the good of all, and absorbed their own losses; explorers opened up the empire and the resources of the unknown world; and the military (for the officer class) represented an heroic, masculine, risk-laden life which – before the mechanized mass butchery of the Great War – had yet to lose its glamour and gloss. For the others, the great mass of people, prosperity might come through hard work and savings, but the main emphasis was on prudent risk avoidance and harm minimization.

The principle of 'risk minimization', as we might now term prudence, appeared in many guises. In the law of accidents, for example, negligence became a major theme. Negligence was defined as not doing what a prudent person would do, or doing what a prudent person would not do. The test of this in common law was the doctrine of 'reasonable foreseeability': which harms should a reasonable person identify as sufficiently likely that precaution should be taken against them? At a time when industry and transportation were growing rapidly, employing many but exposing most of these to the risk of industrial accidents, the law bore harshly on the negligent. An injured worker whose hurt followed from her own negligence, even in a small degree, could not expect to recover compensation. A worker injured by the negligence of a fellow worker could not receive compensation from the employer, but only from the (usually poor) fellow worker. While this meant, in practice, that compensation was largely illusory, and it allowed capital to offload the harmful costs of its development to the public (Horwitz 1977), it was not seen as unjust, at least by the governing classes. Rather it appeared as effective means to risk management – for in both cases it put the workers on their toes in their own interest. Under threat of potentially large financial loss and personal hardship, it made them responsible for their own risks, and thereby disciplined people in the ways of free, rational and independent subjects (O'Malley 2000).

While this may seem to have little to do with crime, for in the twentieth century damages became focused on compensation, civil law in the nineteenth century was much more about punishment (White 2003). Perhaps we could say that damages related to criminal justice penalties in the same allied way that the workhouse related to the prison. Bentham (1962 [1789]), for example, regarded both money damages and fines as punishments, for all that differed in his view was whether money was paid to wronged individuals (damages) or to the wronged state (fines). The punitive law of accidents illustrates an environment in which wrongs and risks were related to each other through a societal lens of rational choice responsibility, manifested particularly in prudence, self-denial, independence and risk avoidance. This makes intelligible the fact that so much criminal justice of the time was directed at 'disreputable pleasures'. Many traditional working-class pleasures now came under suspicion for threatening independence. Some became criminal or were prosecuted more aggressively, notably public drunkenness and certain forms of gambling. As Downes and Davies (1976: 29–32) have shown, the issue of the immorality of gambling was not central to English law until the 1820s. Prior to this, anti-gambling legislation was focused on issues of disorder, excessive gambling and cheating. But during the nineteenth century the theme of gambling as a vice became an increasingly salient problem of national proportions, 'contrary to the civilizing process itself, at the heart of which was the minimization of chance and risk' (Dixon 1991: 49).

Gambling was an assault on the idea of productive labour, on payment for diligence and on the gradual earned accumulation of money saved against a rainy day. Over and above this, by the end of the century new fears were arising associated with the perception that urban life created an unhealthy 'appetite for excitement'. Excitement became a new nervous pathology given its own psychological category of 'neurasthenia', associated with such symptoms as restlessness, inability to concentrate, loss of nerve and depression. Gambling epitomized this urban curse. Quoting a contemporary commentator from the 1890s, Dixon notes that the belief emerged that gambling produced:

> (a)n amount of excitement incompatible with painstaking labour. Excitement unduly indulged in brings about its own penalty in making everything ordinary appear dull, insipid and uninteresting. If working men accustom themselves to sudden gains and losses, they cannot be expected to work steadily at their occupation where the profits are small and the work is hard. (Churchill 1894, quoted by Dixon 1991: 56)

The exceptions made for gambling in middle-class institutions such as gentlemen's clubs, and the fact that public drinking was a working-class rather than middle-class leisure pursuit are suggestive not only of a demand for public order, but also of the policing of pleasures that abused the ideology of prudence and risk avoidance among the economically vulnerable classes (O'Malley and Valverde 2004). In this environment, the pursuit of many traditional pleasures began to take on the character of wilful refusal and opposition. 'Resistance' may be too heroic or romantic a word for the day to day refusal to abandon ways of life and sources of pleasure that did not conform to bourgeois utilitarianism. Nevertheless this was how many of the legal and political discourses of the time envisaged such 'idle' and 'vicious' habits. At best, discourses of 'fecklessness' provided a slightly more forgiving approach, one more open to the interventions of the army of charitable and welfare workers that began to penetrate the lives of ordinary people as the nineteenth century entered its last quarter.

Within this charitable and philanthropic framework, the 'viciousness' of working class ways was in some degree turned into another variety of pathology – all the more so as the twentieth century brought with it a 'social' framework of government that prioritized social factors rather than individual wilfulness as the underlying generators of crime. As David Garland (1985) has stressed, this was not a smooth transition, but an ongoing and unresolved conflict between liberal moralists, who regarded all crime as punishable vice, and those who regarded themselves as 'scientists' of social and individual pathologies that needed expert intervention. What was constant between the two approaches was a view that working class *failure* to embrace deferred gratification and rational calculative prudence was a major factor underlying a considerable bulk of crime. The proponents of the 'social' paradigms advocated an array of explanations for this working-class pathology that were to emerge as the backbone of modern criminology.

'Impulsiveness' and 'short-term hedonism' were attributed to an enormous range of causes that will be familiar to everyone completing Criminology 101. Poor socialization was an early and persistent thesis. Theories varied as to the role of the pathology of single parent families or the impact of parents who were somehow defective in their training skills or who provided bad role models by drinking, unemployment, violence or gambling. Regardless of the variations, the common assumption was that a pathology of socialization had failed to implant 'normal' values and norms that promoted self-denial, deferred gratification, diligence and quiet and private forms of enjoyment. These 'normal' non-hedonistic ways of being, ways that now required the idea of pathology to explain their non-adoption, were just those virtues of risk minimization that Bentham and his cohort, a century before, had struggled to implant into the untamed 'dangerous' classes. The difference was that for Bentham these ways were not natural but part of a yoke of foresight to which naturally 'beastly' people had to become accustomed. Thus what had been a civilizing mission for early liberals, creating new prudential liberal subjects out of a barbarian raw material, had now turned into a mission to recover those who pathologically deviated from a risk-avoiding and precautionary 'normality' that was so taken for granted that now *it* appeared as the natural state.

So much was this the case that other accounts explained the failures to govern through foresight as symptomatic of a throwback to an atavistic, 'pre-Benthamite man'. Either because of limited intelligence, genetic determinism or an abnormality of the central nervous system, they were unable to take on the civilized normality of liberal self-governance. Here the civilizing mission of the early liberals was recognized, but the hedonistic and feckless appeared as a residue of primitivism, people who gave way to impulsiveness, hedonism and even worse vices. More enlightened approaches followed in the wake of these theories. As seen in a previous chapter, the boredom of working-class existence was held responsible for risk-taking behaviours as young men, especially, broke through the constraints that bound them to a prudent life. Young women, more firmly held by the power of the patriarchal family, by implication might have sought the same release from the discipline of risk aversion, but had fewer opportunities and were thus less 'criminal'.

These and many more variations on the theme are accounts now rejected by most critical criminologists. But one of the things these opposing criminologies have in common with each other, as we will soon see, is that they all take for granted the need to explain a deviation from some 'right' level of risk-taking behaviour. Traditional criminologists would locate this right level in some form of prudent activity. Critical criminologists leave this right level completely unstated: but we know they have a problem with the risk-taking search for excitement because it is usually regarded as a response to alienation and lack of control inflicted on us all by late modernity.

Embracing risk

Nothing that has been argued thus far should be taken as a general theory of crime or crime control. I am not talking about all crime, but about the prominent and enduring 'problem' of those crimes imagined to be the consequences of problematic 'irrational' risk-taking among the masses. If most explanations for this have denied the authenticity of risk-taking by pathologizing it, probably the dominant approach for much of the twentieth century, Merton's (1938) 'anomie' or 'strain' theory, accepted the classical criminologists' vision of the rational choice offender. But in contrast to classical criminology's vision of the criminal as an 'everyman' abstracted from social relationships, Merton's sociological criminology posited him (almost certainly a male is in mind) in a structurally disadvantaged position. With access to culturally approved values of wealth and status blocked by poverty, poor education or low social capital, Merton's offenders were envisaged as 'innovating' – that is, as adopting criminal means to achieve the otherwise unattainable prescribed values. Other 'deviants' were variations on this theme. For example, drug users were 'double failures', being envisaged as having failed also at innovative behaviour and opting to 'retreat' into a drug-induced refuge. Considerations of risk are, at best, incidental to this kind of criminology.

While not denying that such theories have some force, in the 1980s Jack Katz (1988) argued that they could not account for one of the most enduring features of crime as reported by offenders themselves: the emotional surge associated with performing criminal acts. With respect to a number of forms of crime, Katz pointed out that offenders are positively attracted to, or seduced by, a 'transcendence' of rationality. Katz's suggestion is that such offenders deliberately allow their calculative rationality to be overtaken by powerful moods in order to overcome some moral challenge to their identity.

With respect to any particular form of crime, the mode and aim of transcendence differs. Probably the easiest to grasp is what Katz refers to as 'sneaky thrills', epitomized by shoplifters, joyriders and vandals. In Katz's account, shoplifting is not so much about economic gain, which often is insignificant. Rather, much offending is engaged in for the excitement that the activity produces. The shoplifter deliberately places herself into a situation of high risk, flirting with the risk of discovery, capture and humiliation. Katz (1988: 312) suggests that the originating thought is that 'it would be so easy' to perform the crime – '"it would be so easy" signals to her not simply that no external obstacles stand firmly in the way, but a secret, internal desire to be deviant'. As the offending is ongoing, time seems to slow down, speed up or disappear as a powerful mood of fear and excitement takes over (Katz 1988: 64). More generally, for Katz, (1988: 312–13) 'young vandals and shoplifters innovate games with the risks of humiliation, running along the edge of shame for its exciting reverberations'.

In this example it can be seen that 'embracing' risk is clearly under-stood to be the source of reward. The shoplifter takes the calculative, mundane prudence that is associated with a liberal morality and common sense, and deliberately overturns it by placing the future at risk. The emotional reward comes both from this exposure to risk and from the sense of achievement at having chanced so much and 'got away with it'. In distinction to Katz, however, it could be suggested that this is neither an escape from rationality or a rejection of rationality, nor an *escape* from anything much. Rather it may be the *positive* pursuit of a rationality in which the rewards are not material but emotional, life is enriched rather than escaped from. But more of this shortly.

Take, as a different example, Katz's analysis of 'righteous slaughter'. Here a person kills out of rage at another who has in some way humiliated him (or occasionally her). Living with humiliation – for example, being cuckolded or publicly belittled – is intolerable. The righteous slayer cannot imagine moving back into the future with any degree of self-respect. He escapes this future by embracing a vision of time-less moral righteousness, envisaging himself as the weapon of vengeance. A moral rage is allowed to sweep over him. 'Rage is mercifully blind to the future' because it 'focuses consciousness on the here and now' (Katz 1988: 30–1); and so the subject escapes unbearable mundane reality.

Street robbery and street fighting, as another example, are associated by Katz with the sorts of working class and slum areas that are the prime objects of Merton's anomie theory. In this instance, Katz does not so much deny the 'structural' inequality and blocked opportunities to wealth and success that concern Merton; rather he sees the motivation for action as arising out of the humiliation of the situation. Katz regards the 'arrogant postures of domination' associated with street fighters and others, as 'elicited' by the structurally induced sense of humiliation which is then 'reacted against and obliterated by the emotions generated by situations of anger, aggression and danger'(Katz 1988: 12).

What holds all these different crime scenarios together for Katz is a narrow band of emotions. He suggests that:

> Running across these experiences of criminality is a process juxtaposed in one manner or another by humiliation. In committing righteous slaughter, the impassioned assailant takes humiliation and turns it into rage ... The badass with searing purposefulness, tries to scare humiliation off ... young vandals and shoplifters innovate games with risks of humiliation, running along the edge of shame for its exciting reverberations. Fashioned as street elites, young men square off against the increasingly humiliating social restrictions of childhood by mythologising differences with other groups of young men. (1988: 312–13)

Why is humiliation so central in Katz's account? Perhaps it is because he seeks in it a commonality between rather diverse crimes. If we move away from his concern with arguing for the importance of emotional experience as opposed to rationality (a problematic binary in any case) it is not difficult to perceive that the righteous slayer is quite distinct from the shoplifter or joyrider. They differ in motivation, in their relationship with humiliation, in the emotion or mood they seek to be generated, in the imagined relationship between their present action and the imagined future, and so on. More particularly for our purposes, only some of these offenders are risk-takers. Risk does not seem to be at issue with the righteous slayers: they are not seeking either to take risks or, thereby, to experience a thrill.

Given my focus on crime and risk-taking, it becomes both possible and sensible to separate these forms of 'emotionally' driven crime and focus only on the risk-takers – for again, the aim is not to understand all crime. With the shoplifter, Katz posits flirting with risks of humiliation as the generator of thrills. But surely there are many things other than (or as well as) humiliation 'at risk': the risk of losing money through fines, of receiving other punishment such as probation and perhaps imprisonment, the risk to one's future job prospects, maybe the risk of a physical beating from an irate parent. It could equally be argued that what generates excitement here is *fear*. Taking risks, at least in the present, is intelligible as a source of excitement in part because of the adrenaline rush released by a kind of vertigo – of being on an edge where one's future existence itself seems at stake. The same applies, perhaps, with the example of young men confronting other young men in street fights. It is quite plausible to suggest that it is not the humiliation of life in the barrios that is the issue, but rather the opportunity for excitement associated with the risk of pain or injury, even death, mixed perhaps with an excited liking for inflicting these fearful possibilities (Jackson-Jacobs 2004).

'Control', edgework and the critical pathology of risk-taking

Linked with this source of excitement, Katz, and more recently writers examining the phenomenon of 'edgework' (Lyng 1991, 2005) raise a second sensation pertinent to crimes that embrace risk. With respect to shoplifters, Katz notes that 'usually after the scene of risk is successfully exited ... (another) stage of the sneaky thrill is realized ... In one form or another, there is a "Wow I got away with it!" or an "It was so easy!" (Katz 1988: 64). Risk-taking produces a positive reward alongside the thrill induced by fear of loss: a sense of having succeeded in a difficult and consequential task; a sense of achievement at having been at the limits of chaos and managing to survive through one's ability to control the situation. This is the side of things most emphasized in Lyng's (1991, 2005) analysis of 'edgework' as the 'risk-taking experience'. For Katz, examples such as the righteous slayer slip in and out of control, or seek in some ways to lose control in order to escape from humiliation and enter a timeless zone. For the edgework literature, however, maintaining control is a key part of the reward structure. Again this suggests a need to differentiate some of Katz's examples – particularly the shoplifters, vandals, joyriders and street fighters – from others such as the 'righteous slaughterer'. Edgeworkers are said to gain a lasting satisfaction through the authentication of the self and its competence: the ability to 'control', rather than seeking refuge in the loss of control. Other forms of offending, such as graffiti writing, the theft and destruction of cars, fire starting, vandalism, burglary, street fighting and cheque fraud, 'juvenile delinquency', drug taking and finance crime have all been examined in the light of risk-seeking for the edgeworking thrills they produce (for example, Denton 2001, Hayward 2004: 153, Miller 2005, Reith 2005, Smith 2005, Halsey 2008).

One of the principal contributions of Lyng's focus on the excitement produced by achievement has been to emphasize that 'voluntary risk-taking', and the thrills that it generates, are not restricted to criminal activity or to those who in some sense fail to cope with mundane rationality. Lyng's own work has emphasized high-risk sports such as sky diving, hang gliding, rock climbing and so on. Edgework thus links risk-taking crime with risk-taking more generally, enabling analysis to escape some of the limitations of the criminological theorizing that regards crime as requiring unique explanations. Unfortunately, however, much of the ensuing analysis resurrects the pathological vision of risk-taking that has dogged criminology.

Lyng himself (1991, 2005: 5–6) starts the ball rolling by regarding edgework as compensation or escape from an alienating existence produced by modern society, with 'intense sensations of self-determination and self-control thus providing an escape from the structural conditions supporting alienation and oversocialization'. It is a theme that is picked up by Miller (2005: 166–7) who suggests that 'an edgework model of delinquency suggests that constraining social institutions may give rise to alienation. Delinquency can provide an authentic, exciting way for some adolescents to escape their otherwise routine and alienating lives'. The engagement in edgework, whether legitimate or criminal, thus appears as making up for a deficit in existence produced by late modern society. It is eerily similar to Miller's (1958) namesake criminologist, who regarded working-class crime as generated by the boredom and powerlessness of working-class existence.

Other criminologists, however, have suggested that this focus on the routine and mundane nature of the modern world needs to be given a more specific context. Keith Hayward (2004: 154–6), for example, argues insightfully that such developments may be linked to a broader setting of late modernity in which questions of uncertainty and insecurity have become endemic. He quotes, with qualified approval, Jock Young who states that:

> We live now in a much more difficult world: we face a greater range of life choices than even before, our lives are less firmly embedded in work and relationships, our everyday existence is experienced as a series of encounters with risk either in actuality or in the shape of fears and apprehensions. We feel both materially insecure and ontologically precarious. (Young 1999: vi)

More recently, Young (2007: 12) has pushed this further to suggest that 'vertigo is a malaise of modern society: a sense of insecurity, of insubstantiality, and of uncertainty, a whiff of chaos and a fear of falling'. This is also a common interpretation of the ethos of the risk society promoted by such theorists as Beck (1992) and Giddens (1994). From this basis, Hayward adopts what amounts to a revised alienation thesis. In the current uncertain context, he suggests individuals feel powerless, and powerlessness is linked to the desire to take control. Thus Hayward seeks to move beyond Katz's argument that crime 'is seductive because of the excitement it brings at the level of subjective experience, and to look instead at how crime represents, for many, a way both of seizing control and expressing identity' (Hayward 2004: 155).

Again, there is a critical development here, for Hayward is identifying a plausible hypothesis about how voluntary risk-taking may be understood. But I want to question how far such risk-taking is to do with alienation, powerlessness and loss of control. Rather than posit a pathology of loss of control experienced by 'late modernity', I would argue that the changes with which we are concerned have a rather longer history and it is this to which attention needs to be directed. In this light, is it really plausible to suggest that people now feel more powerless than when under the threat of nuclear devastation by superpowers in the 1950s, or when their lives were catastrophically disrupted by two World Wars separated by a devastating global depression and preceded by another depression in the 1890s – often forgotten but far more severe in its effects on everyday life than the financial crisis beginning in 2008? Couldn't it be argued with at least equal plausibility that in the long half century after World War II things improved? Arguably, the longest and most spectacular period of economic boom coupled with the gradual retreat of the Cold War, to say nothing of the remarkable expansion of welfare states, may have produced a *decrease* in feelings of insecurity and powerlessness compared to any comparable period in modern experience?

In the generally prosperous post-war environment the hold of the nineteenth-century ethos of individual prudence and self-denial was weakened precisely because people were *freed up* in specific ways by economic, cultural and political conditions. Summed up in the idea of the consumer society, what is indisputably novel is that in this period far more people than ever before had the opportunity to take part in a culture in which voluntary risk-taking became practicable, desirable and reasonable.

Katz, Lyng and others do report empirical evidence that those offenders and others doing voluntary risk-taking assert that control, as well as excitement is an important component of the emotional response they seek. This is important. But why should that imply a deficit that needs to be *compensated* by this performance? Why, to use a *deliberately* gendered term, might the emphasis on control not simply be reflecting the thrill of mastery coupled with the thrill of taking risks? Rather than positing a pathology of alienation and powerlessness that, by implication, needs correcting, embracing risk could be quite the reverse – a positive achievement that enhances an ordinary (not a deficient) life? Would it be the case, for example, that a capitalist pulling off a risky but highly successful enterprise would be regarded as alienated, suffering from a control deficit in his or her life? Were explorers and adventurers in the nineteenth century battling with the insecurities generated by the risk society? I don't think so. Perhaps the democratization of such positive risk-taking into 'edgework' performed by many rather than an elite has been misunderstood as a 'problem'. Maybe, instead, edgework could be seen as the broadening of access to such thrills, produced by (among other changes) the rise of consumer society? At least in its commodified forms, it may be an improvement in our lot – an array of newly available excitements, if only for those in the market, rather than a symptom of a new social pathology?

At the other end of the scale, did young men get involved in street fights in the slums of nineteenth century Sydney and New York because of ontological insecurity and powerlessness (or for that matter humiliation)? Or were they taking opportunities for excitement that were generally refused to them as legitimate activities in a society of self-denial? Couldn't it be that they would find mastery and control thrilling just as people do today? In sum, I suspect the current explanations of edgework, including those that apply the concept to criminal activity, may be under-estimating the extent to which this existed in the past, and wrongly pathologizing the legitimated avenues for edgework that have appeared in the present.

These might be seemingly flip rhetorical questions, but their point is very serious. It is being assumed in much of the literature reviewed here that risk-taking and the thrills it delivers are abnormal, or at best a normal response to an abnormal situation. This perversely continues the nineteenth-century moral dogma that assumes risk aversion is optimal or 'normal', albeit that it promotes this argument in a form that does not condemn the subjects. Suppose, however, what has changed since the nineteenth century is neither the nature or wellsprings of excitement generated by risk-taking, nor the level of subjective control experienced in everyday life. Rather, maybe what has changed is the social distribution of these activities, and the cultural forms they take. To sketch out my argument, could it be that what separates current risk takers from their nineteenth century forebears is that many more people, running across the class, gender and race lines that were formerly barriers to such things, are now legitimately engaged in these sorts of activity? If so, perhaps this is not because people are more alienated and ontologically insecure nowadays, but rather because many more people are more 'free' to govern their own risks than was the case a century, or even a half century ago. In turn, perhaps this new environment changes the meanings, if not necessarily the prevalence, of crimes that 'embrace risk'.

Risky freedoms

This argument rests on several foundations. To begin with, there has been a cultural shift away from a blanket regime of risk aversion and dutiful prudence toward one in which room is made for self-fulfilment.

Self-fulfilment through pleasure and excitement – including approved forms of risk-taking – have become acceptable, even necessary, to a well rounded 'lifestyle' in liberal mainstream culture. Closely linked to this, the means to achieve such excitements have been commodified and thus made more accessible to many in a consumer society: the flawed democracy of the market place. Many of the examples of edgework highlighted by Lyng – skydiving, base jumping, extreme mountaineering – take the form of expensive commodities. In some degree this was true in the past, but the equivalent activities, including mountaineering expeditions, were restricted to a tiny minority by the enormous costs involved, let alone by normative barriers. Now, these and less risky (or less spectacular) thrills are routinely present in the everyday life of many, and have been morphed into the virtual edgework of computer games that occupy the leisure time of vast numbers.

No doubt linked to capital's need to create ever-renewing markets, the rise of consumer society was linked to the shaping of a demand for novelty and change. But it is also arguable that the conditions of urban life themselves stimulated an acceptance that episodes of excitement should be a reasonable expectation for most citizens. As noted above, a 'crisis' emerged as early as the 1890s over the fact that urban life created 'excitement', and phantasms of 'neurasthenia' made themselves visible even to sophisticated social theorists such as Georg Simmel (1990 [1895]) who believed urban dwellers became disoriented by the ephemeral and frenetic life of the city. Such 'crises' registered the first glimmerings of a dawn that gradually broke through the night of a culture dominated by utilitarianism, risk avoidance and self-discipline. Values, beliefs and practices that had never successfully been extirpated by the ethos of prudence and the glorification of the Protestant Ethic, were fanned back into public life, even if held in check by the austere realities of two world wars and a depression (Cross 1993). Affirmations of self-gratification and self-fulfilment through hedonism had been given intellectual expression by the nineteenth century Romantic movement that identified the 'real' self with an emotional and expressive refusal of liberal utilitarianism. But most likely the key sources of mass change were resilient wellsprings and cultures of pleasure among the mass of the (urban) population that had been the target of so much nineteenth and early twentieth century moral reform – a moral movement that had been so noisy and insistent precisely because of the success of resistance to it (O'Malley and Mugford 1994).

This suggests that the rise of consumer society drew upon a *resistance* to prudent risk minimization and the grey world this created – a resistance that drove a large bulk of 'popular' crime in the nineteenth century. If novelty and excitement emerged as key forms of commodified pleasure during and after the 1950s, this was not simply invented by capital and pressed upon a malleable and alienated populace. It drew on and released a suppressed demand for a life that to a greater extent embraced risk, excitement and pleasure. In short, risk-taking is no more but no less 'natural' and 'healthy' than risk-aversion: we do not need to resort to explanations in terms of powerlessness and alienation or some other pathology to explain the embrace of risk in the late modern world. It is surprising to many modern theorists only to the extent that prudent risk-aversion, the creation of nineteenth century liberals, had become legitimated as 'normal'.

Of course the impact of this shift can be exaggerated. The risk-managerial welfare state has run interference throughout the twentieth century. It created all manner of technologies that 'explain' the pathology of short-run hedonism. Aided and abetted by positivist criminology it gave a seemingly amoral scientific gloss to the normality and necessity of deferred gratification and self-denial. But by the 1960s even this was beginning to be challenged; on the political Left by those opposed to 'technocratic' domination by the social professions, and more importantly on the Right, by free market neo-liberals. It is the latter, during the 1970s and 1980s, who referred to the welfare state as the 'no risk society' (Aharoni 1984), and began a project of valorizing risk-taking and enterprise as an essential element of the active subject. From the early 1980s forward, risk-taking began to appear not merely as acceptable but as a positive good, and even the duty of liberal subjects. As Rose (1999) has pointed out, individuals were to become 'entrepreneurs of themselves', investing on the stock markets and property markets, taking 'control' of their futures by shifting their savings from defined benefit pensions to market-driven schemes, leaving 'dead end' jobs, starting small enterprises and so on. The contours of this manoeuvre, together with the cruel illusions it fostered and the illiberalities it inflicted on those who 'failed' in this entrepreneurial world, are now clear. But if the rise of the consumer society made it acceptable to become more risk adventurous, at least through commodified means, the neo-liberal revolution made it a *duty for all*.

The reverse side of this neo-liberal risk coinage was the 'responsibilization' strategy: the downloading to individuals of the responsibility to manage all manner of harmful risks that previously had been assigned, at least in principal, to the risk management of the welfare state. In no way did this 'revised prudentialism' (O'Malley 1992) contradict the vision of the enterprising society. Rather, in a significant transformation of nineteenth century liberalism, the idea was that individuals would choose that level of risk exposure they preferred, buying private insurances to suit their own desires for health, property, income, employment or old age security. If we do feel more insecure than before, in considerable measure this is a deliberate effect of these policies. We are 'more free' in such a sense, and it's worth remembering that the Left too railed against the stifling intrusiveness of the interventionist state. But the spur of insecurity is what neo-liberals, whose politics swamped those of the Left, imagined would drive subjects to take best advantage of the risk-taking opportunities offered by the new 'freedom of choice'.

In turn, this revised approach to risk released any lingering brake provided by an economy of self-denial and thrift. Self-fulfilment and self-gratification through the market became Good Things. In place of a thrifty discipline of self-denial emerged what Featherstone (1994) has referred to as a 'controlled hedonism'. The risky world of the market rewarded the successful with commodified pleasures. Those who succeeded in the new normality of enterprise society could, within far more relaxed moral perimeters than before, legitimately buy the pleasures and excitements they desired. As Jonathan Simon (2002) has argued, in such an environment of government-sanctioned, get-rich-quick, risk-embracing opportunism it is not so surprising that extreme excitements have moved from the preserve of a very few to the purchasable expectation of the many.

Certainly this transition in practice has been uneven in its reach. The same was true for the risk-minimizing ideology that preceded it. But among other significant changes occurring is that popular risky pleasures have moved out from the shadowy world of illicit or illegal practices that were formerly expressions of resistance against the culture of prudence. Gambling probably is the most obvious of these. Under the rubric of a new 'leisure industry', lauded for the employment it creates, the revenues it generates for the state, and for the entertainment it provides, gambling has become a legitimate feature of everyday life. It is now even possible to become a 'responsible gambler', alongside 'responsible drinkers' and so on (O'Malley 2004). This appears not simply in the growing world of casinos, where the distinction between a respectable night's entertainment and gambling has disappeared. Nor just in the betting shops, where – through such devices as betting on the stock market – the distinction between gambling and business speculation has become completely blurred. Even more so, it is in the daily televized presentations of sweepstakes, lotteries and keno, the news items created as the winning pools pass into the tens of millions of dollars. And it is ubiquitously available in the online betting games that create a world of risk-embracement in the suburban living room.

Risk-embracing crimes and subterranean risk-taking

Crime has lurked somewhat in the background of this analysis. Nevertheless if we are to understand the nexus between risk and the performance of crime, it is essential to see how risk is contextualized and what meanings and material effects are assigned to it. Before elaborating, let me stress again that I am not arguing that risk-embracing crime is new. So what is new? I suggest three things: the nature of some offences that are linked to the pursuit of excitement through embracing risk (not necessarily the *volume* of risk-embracing crimes); the meanings of such offences to offenders and others; and the structural explanations that might be offered for these kinds of crime.

To the extent that risk-taking has migrated to being a mainstream value, many of the offences that embrace risk have themselves moved from being a form of resistance to being a form of conformity. This is despite the fact that many such offences are acts of defiance or even, on occasions, acts of protest. What I am suggesting is that the criminal action is no longer in opposition to a current culture of risk, as were many working-class pleasure crimes typified by gambling. By and large, gambling has disappeared as a class crime simply through acts of legislation, and that particular underground criminal economy of popular excess has largely been obliterated. Insofar as this was a major form of working-class offending, both for operators and customers, then we should not automatically assume that risk-embracing crime has increased in volume in the past 50 years or so: it may even have declined.

Running against this important, if little recognized, consideration is the fact that changes in the legitimate economy of excitement have created new risk-embracing forms of offending. Street car racing, more often than not with the offenders' own vehicles and often organized in 'meets' of some scale, has developed with the increased accessibility and availability of high performance vehicles (Vaaranen 2004). The growth of the 'bikie' gang, centred on expensive, high powered and 'chopped' machines embraces the joy of risk-taking even though it may often be linked to a routine business culture of illicit drug distribution. Rave parties, binge drinking and the ecstasy and 'recreational' drug cultures that have grown up around the night club scene, represent forms of risky excitement that are distinguished from more 'traditional' cultures of illicit drug consumption centred on opiates (for example, Measham 2004, Hayward and Hobbs 2007). Each of these is not just explicitly or borderline criminal, they also rely on the performers being embedded in the culture of consumption, and relatively successfully so. Using the term developed by David Matza (1964) many years ago, these represent 'subterranean' forms of offending, crimes that in key ways conform to mainstream values but express or perform them in legally problematic ways.

Even so, to label such crimes subterranean, and thus 'conforming', conceals key differences among them. For some, there is – to use another of Matza's (1964) terms – a process of 'drift' into crime in which it is relatively easy to cross the border from legality into crime precisely because the border is made vague by cultural shifts or ambiguities. This is readily intelligible where high-risk activities are valorized by legitimate industries. Binge drinking is one instance. But the same is true of white-collar crimes. The infamous Nick Leeson episode is a case in point. Massive debts were incurred by a financial trader who was eventually imprisoned for financial irregularities sufficient to bring down an important investment bank. Yet debts were allowed to build up in good measure because the environment of high risk financial trading 'pushing the envelope' was good practice. The borderline between legitimate risk-taking and criminal recklessness is sufficiently fluid that specialist professions have grown up around its policing (Halliday 2004), and in Leeson's case – while later it came to be obvious that criminality was involved – the precise point at which this line was crossed is hard to define.

In other offending of the subterranean type, however, the idea of conformity in some respects may conceal a considerable degree of resistance. As Michel de Certeau (1985) has argued, because we live our lives so much through commodities, the commodities are adapted to many of the purposes that were once the preserve of other actions. Many varieties of popular culture express explicit resistance to some mainstream political and cultural values and practices through dress, music, body decoration, hair styles, drugs, cars and motor cycles. In some of these cases, notably drugs and vehicles, the commodities are the means or medium through which criminal offending is performed.

Each of these patterns of risk-embracing crime in some way may be interpreted as 'liberated' by the consumer revolution and the neo-liberal political turn. For all the appalling political and economic harms these developments may have created, they have liberated the lives of a significant portion of the population from the dour discipline of self-denial and thrift. It was a dour life no less (likely more) alienating or out of the control of ordinary people than is life in the present. But the 'freedom of choice' that has been delivered is mediated through the democracy of the market at a time when, since the 1980s at least, wealth has been polarizing. The situation is one that creates structurally-based anomie in Merton's sense of a strain between core societal values accepted by the many and legitimate access to the means of achieving them (Young 2007: 48–51).

Yet, as Keith Hayward suggests (2004: 161), this is not just Merton's instrumental model in which material wealth is the generalized goal. In a commodified neo-liberal world, in which stimulation and excitement through risk-taking are valorized, money is still the legitimated means to (commodified) self-fulfilment. For many, this is enough, at least when linked to symbolic issues associated with status, success and the like (Hall et al. 2008). But for many other offenders it is the blocked access to legitimate forms of excitement, rather than just the wealth and symbolic value itself, that leads to Mertonian innovative behaviour. If a valued goal is excitement and self-fulfilment, and risk-taking is a means to achieve this, then for some people the question would become 'Why not by-pass the market and move directly to the desired commodities?'. One of the most obvious examples is car stealing and joyriding. Thus in Mark Halsey's (2008) research on car crime as edgework, car theft was not so much about any chance of making money, but rather the thrill – which was heightened further if police gave chase. Things could hardly have been made clearer than by one of the joyriders:

> *Interviewer*: ... you know, I understand people want to get a thrill and all that sort of thing. Why not go skydiving or why not do this or that?
>
> *Participant*: You need money to do that though don't you?...
>
> *Interviewer*: Yeah sure.
>
> *Participant*: They say there's heaps of things to do but fuckin' where are you meant to get the money for it? Centrelink [i.e. the government unemployment centre]? Two hundred bucks a fuckin' fortnight? Where does that go? Fuck all. (Halsey 2008: 112)

This does not seem like an escape from humiliation or alienation, but a simple problem that Merton understood as well as Katz, perhaps better. If the societal value you have adopted is excitement, if excitement is commodified and you cannot be in the market for it, then resort to illegal means to embrace risky commodities.

Diversity and risk, diversity of risk

Many years ago, Eleanor Miller (1991) objected to the focus on edgework to the extent that it ignored other kinds of risks and other experiences of risk. Miller pointed to the fact, discussed in the previous chapter, that for most women, exposure to risk associated with gendered and sexualized violence is more salient and significant than thrill seeking. However, the danger in focusing only on such defensive approaches to risk is that women can be reduced to victims, to subjects who are risk aversive rather than people who will take risks willingly in pursuit of desired ends. As Sandra Walklate pointed out, 'women unquestionably seek pleasure, excitement, thrills and risks. How and under what circumstances this occurs, however, has been explored relatively infrequently, and when it has it has often been pathologized. Women are, after all, the "Other"; typically defined as being outside the discourse of risk and risk seeking ...' (1997: 43).

There is now no shortage of research demonstrating that women can and do embrace risk for much the same purposes as do men. Barbara Denton's (2001) work among women who run drug networks, for example, described many situations in which criminal activities were valued as much or more for their emotional thrill as for the material gains. Frequently engaged in credit card fraud and passing dud cheques, these women described the excitement generated by facing the risk of discovery by pulling off the crime, often facing down the distrust of the bank teller. For these women, mostly with criminal records, there was no flirting with humiliation. Rather it was the more tangible consequence of imprisonment that gave the actions their edge, coupled with the fact that they experienced the excitement of being in control of the edge of disaster. In this much, they gained thrills in identical ways to their male equivalents.

However, things may also be more nuanced. Rajah's (2007) work among drug users found that African-American and Puerto Rican women with habitually violent male partners gain satisfaction from seemingly minor forms of resistance that risk a violent response. Knowing at what point to pull back from a confrontation, carrying out small acts of revenge, manipulating the subtleties of power that allow room for open defiance, are all examples Rajah shows to generate a thrill of satisfaction through the ability to control life on the edge. Often these are complex relational manoeuvres. Thus one of the women, Ciara, reported that when invited to his apartment by a sexually attractive drug dealer, she deliberately flaunted this act of sexual resistance in the face of her partner judging that his fear of the dealer would likely restrain a violent, possibly lethal response. Another woman, Louisa, would resist her partner's sexual overtures and then 'all of a sudden when he least expected it boom. I would just whip it on him and it would be over with'. As Rajah notes,

> the thrill and pleasure derived by both Louisa and Ciara derives in part because both women believed their partners had levels of awareness that they were being thwarted. While this made the risks they were taking

real, both women counted on their partner's not responding with violence because doing so would acknowledge the emasculating defiance and illuminate the men's tenuous control ... [Their acts] expressed a sense of accomplishment and personal authorship that are the ultimate goal of successful edgework. (Rajah 2007: 208–09)

Thus, to argue that there are circumstances in which women's risk-taking crime is not specifically gendered, as with Denton's drug dealers, should not cover up the possibility that gender does shape risk-taking in important ways. Katz (1988: 246–7) himself pointed out that men's risk-taking crimes can be understood in terms of 'distinctively male forms of action and ways of being' such as collective fighting, drinking and gambling.

There may be still more to the gendering of risks even than this suggests. Sandra Walklate (1997), for example, has raised the possibility that the desire for control may be a highly gendered value, and that for this reason alone risk itself, as a source or means of control, may be a gendered category. It may be that for women more frequently than for men, deliberately exposing oneself to risks may have as its aim the expression of trust and the fostering of emotional relationships in which excitements of the sort mentioned so far have no great part, and control still less so. Thus Rhodes' (1997: 220) research with female sex workers found that 'constraints on some women's attempts at condom negotiation were particularly evident when the negotiation of unprotected sex was perceived as carrying with it greater risks than unprotected sex'. For these women, suggesting the use of a condom would mean that the relationship would suffer; the emotional value of this love warranted the risks taken. Kane Race (2007), in his study of gay men, likewise found that deliberately exposing oneself to the risk of HIV infection had much more to do with caring about the relationship, and the implications of condom use, than any stereotypical vision of unprotected and risky gay sex being more exciting. While it is a very 'unmasculine' concept in social science, love – which is both thrilling and exciting in its own distinctive ways – may be as important a motivator for embracing risks as the thrills generated by running along the edge of fear, or the joy found in manifesting control.

Much of the edgework and related literature emphasizing lack of control as a hidden motive for taking risks may thus reflect a particular 'macho' masculine perspective. Without producing yet another gender binary, women may more frequently than men find other rewards more important, and may not regard as thrilling what edgeworkers regard as excitement-driven risk-taking. Indeed, Marsha Rosenbaum has argued that:

> Men and women differ in their attitude toward risk. For male addicts, particularly at the beginning of their career with heroin or at the beginning of each new run, the daily overcoming of risk and chaos makes this life exciting and alluring ... heroin is deemed a rewarding feeling for a hard half-day's work ... [however] on a subjective level, women disdain the riskiness of the heroin lifestyle. It is not surprising that women derive no positive status from engaging in risk. (1981: 50)

Susan Batchelor (2007) found that matters were more complicated still in her study of Scots women offenders. Younger women often adopted stereotypical 'female' risk-avoiding postures because of the influence of dominant cultural expectations. But others, whom she called 'street fighters', did seek out risks for the thrills produced, while many older women regarded such activities as a source of shame and embarrassment. As Hannah-Moffat and O'Malley (2007: 24) conclude in their review of such research, gender, class, age, race and ethnicity produce such crucial effects at the level of experience that many of the general theorizations of edgework and risk-taking crime may need to be re-thought.

This does not mean that because of such diversity the analysis of the changing place of excitement and risk-taking in late modernity and neo-liberal governance has to be abandoned. There is too much evidence that risk-taking has become a prominent and positively evaluated cultural and political form to discard the proposition. Understanding the crime and risk-taking nexus is more important than ever before. However, social theory may have been too ready to read-off certain effects of this shift, as if it has a more or less fixed and consistent character across diverse populations, and as if it can be deduced from theoretically driven analysis alone. The first half of this book argued that it is important not to essentialize risk-minimizing governmental strategies and techniques, to think of the often repressive form they have taken as the only form they could take. Risk minimization may be put to a variety of political purposes and causes other than those recognized in the bulk of criminology. I am now suggesting that the same is true – and with much the same significance – for the *experience* of risk, with similar political implications. If risk-taking means different things to different people, then this has to be taken into account when developing ways of dealing with risk-taking crime in the twenty-first century.

Changes in the cultural and political place and meaning of risk-taking distance the contemporary world of public and popular morality from that of the years prior to World War II, and especially from the nineteenth century. The impact this has had on experience and action is unlikely to be uniform. In part, this may reflect opportunity structures. Legitimate avenues for risk-taking are shaped by class, gender, race and so on. In part, it may also reflect more deeply embedded cultural differences that influence what is valued in life, that filter, valorize, erase, reshape and otherwise translate the publicly salient ideas of risk-taking and risk-minimizing. Some commentators (for example, Hayward 2004) have pointed out that risk-taking and excitement are possibly integral to terrorism, with one implication being that, within certain contexts, formally criminalized risk-taking takes on a positive religious and/or political value. It is critical to recognize that changing official discourses on risk-taking have gone hand-in-hand with other shifts in almost every area of life (not least the rise of the women's movement and multiculturalism) that affect these evaluations. The salience of risk-taking in the present means that we must face the fact that a politics of risk in criminal justice and crime control must also include a politics of the meanings and experience of risk-taking. It is to this issue that the final chapter turns.

FOUR

a risk-taking criminology

Critical criminology is deep in one of its more pessimistic phases, beset by a culture of control in which constraining risk techniques perform an ever more intrusive and negative role. There is a lot of truth in this vision of criminal justice, and there is no point ignoring the obvious. On the other hand, there is also no point in criminologists simply cataloguing each new risk-based retreat from progressive criminal justice and confirming the hopelessness of the situation. We have seen already that in the belly of the neo-liberal, crime-controlling beast there are risk-based techniques that could provide a platform for a more positive, if nevertheless 'dangerous', approach to the governance of crime. Drug harm minimization, risk-needs-responsivity and developmental crime prevention provide some positive potentials and object lessons worth considering as resources for creating a more positive criminal justice than the 'culture of control' theorists envisage as our likely future.

In this final chapter I will explore some lines of flight offered by developments in justice, although not by returning in detail to these examples whose possibilities have already been flagged. Instead I want to turn to two rather different risk-related developments that I think may become increasingly important in the future: fines and monetary sanctions more generally, and community crime prevention and community justice. In a world in which an advanced liberal governmentality is still king, these offer opportunities for engagement with existing crime control on a terrain that is politically plausible. Both of these, separately and together, have an uncertain promise that an optimistic, risk-taking criminology could engage with. Each is already substantially in place as a major element of justice and may already be pointing us toward new and possibly coexisting futures.

At the same time, many contemporary criminologists have tended to regard cultures of risk-taking crime with considerable ambivalence and sometimes pessimism. Offenders who embrace risks are frequently made to appear as narcissistic products of an alienated and insecure late modern risk society. Yet I have argued that many of the risk-embracing crimes of excitement are not forms of escapism from a pathological world, nor compensations for a powerless and alienated existence. In the course of modern history, people – nice, nasty and mostly in between – have refused to abandon their risky ways of life in the face of moralizing and technocratic government. There is cause for (always qualified) optimism here too. Criminalized forms of sexual diversity, drug-taking, drinking and gambling have become risky no-man's-lands in which moral tolerance is constantly being stretched, and decriminalization advanced. Hand-in-hand with this, the commercialization of almost everything has provided an environment that has aided and abetted the erosion of self-denying risk minimization. More surprising and unexpected than any of this was the arrival of neo-liberal politics bearing its faith in markets as regulators and its aversion to a 'paternalistic state'. This provided further impetus in the direction of what neo-liberals call 'freedom of choice' – albeit that its own sometimes illusory nature and frequent appropriation by neo-conservatives have made this a patchy, qualified and unpredictable advance.

One way of putting these two developments together would be to envision a 'coming crisis' in which a culture valorizing the embrace of risk collides with a crime control system that is built around a concern with risk minimization. It is possible, but it's hard to see the future this way. Rather than one big bang, I think Deleuze (1995: 172–3) had a better handle on things when he suggested that 'any society is defined not so much by its contradictions as by its lines of flight, it flees all over the place, and it's very interesting to try to follow the lines of flight taking shape at some particular moment or other'. One aspect of this was Deleuze's idea of nomadism – that if restrictions are removed people will head off in surprising directions limited only by imagination and the resources at hand. Another is that governing lines themselves are remarkably labile and inventive and constantly generate unanticipated consequences and opportunities. Thus once people were made 'responsible' for their own risks after the 1970s, it wasn't long before governments began to generate 'responsible drinkers', 'responsible gamblers' and even 'responsible drug takers'. Victorians would have had conniptions at such moral license! Of course this 'responsibilizes' these risky pleasures into something like a good behaviour bond. But compared to the stifling moral regimes that preceded it, it is an historical release into our own custody. More important, it is decidedly ambiguous, ambivalent, probably unstable and likely to morph into something else before too long. It is a platform from which to act innovatively. The potential for promoting other kinds of freedom and tolerance, and for pressing back against an encroachment of cramping risk minimization does not seem so hard to imagine. Maybe criminology should embrace some risks and weigh in to the process by looking for opportunities, keeping an eye out for the lines of flight – rather than focusing only on the negative trends, the obstacles to progress and the risks of experimentation. Risk technologies lend themselves to a politics of opportunity not just because they are relatively new and still fizzing, but because risk has *two* potentialities that criminological theorists have identified – an encroaching and a tolerant governmentality – even if only the former has preoccupied them.

The familiar direction is that of risk-encroaching on life. As new risks are discovered, as new risk-measuring techniques are invented, and as new ways for reducing risks are devised, so more and more of life is governed in terms of a future that is only *possible*. A whole array of pre-emptive measures – such as Serious Crime Prevention Orders and Anti-Social Behaviour Orders in Britain – have been introduced in the grey zone between civil and criminal law. They intervene in actions that are 'not yet' criminal. They license intervention on the basis of probabilistic risk factors alone, yet ironically even though (or because) no past offence is at issue, the protection of criminal procedure is relaxed (Zedner 2009: 84–5). Obviously these kinds of 'culture of control' examples are more than worrying, even where they may appear justified (Ashworth and Zedner forthcoming). But not all risk-based developments are necessarily to be viewed with such dismay.

The less familiar way of characterizing risk, as Simon (1988) has noted, is that risk has an enormous potential for tolerance. Whereas discipline is focused on closed institutions and shaping individuals into conformity with a norm, risk technologies may simply work to police security boundaries – leaving the space within relatively open and morally floating. Essentially, governance through markets and commodities works this way. Commodities are risk assessed before being distributed – but within this 'policed' perimeter of risk, consumers are free to select the lifestyle, moralities and ethics of their choice. Furthermore, within the flawed democracy of the market place, governance can be effected by regulation of prices – discouraging but not prohibiting unwanted activity. Tobacco and alcohol consumption are examples. As free marketeers such as Milton Friedman (1994) have argued, this would be a far better way to regulate illicit drugs than to drive them and their effects into the unregulated zone of criminal supply and use. Decriminalization coupled with regulation of supply, taxation and harm minimization represent a way out of the War on Drugs that could hardly be more devastating.

The stress on pricing risky and criminal activities, through taxation, licensing, premiums and so on, has much to recommend it in a commodified society increasingly characterized by a high value placed on risk-taking. But of course, such pricing mechanisms aside, it is already the case that monetary sanctions – in the form of fines, restitution orders, damages, costs and so on – effectively render the vast majority of justice into exactly such a pricing mechanism – and, I will argue, one that is effectively based on risk.

Commodified sanctions

Although it has escaped almost everyone's attention, fines have long operated as the principal technique of governing crimes through risk. In most jurisdictions outside the US, fines make up about 70 per cent of court dispositions (O'Malley 2009a). Furthermore, fines are the principal sanction used against corporations and government departments and agencies. And towering over everything is the enormous bulk of regulatory and administrative fines – often flowing into criminal justice – typified by fines related to traffic offences and infringements. We should add to this, the use of civil damages as a crime-linked sanction. In the US, especially, legislation allows for treble damages to be awarded, and facilitates civil actions, as an adjunct to conviction and fines in egregious cases of corporate and organized crime.

It seems likely that one of the reasons why criminology has almost ignored fines, with very few exceptions (Rusche and Kirchheimer 1939, Bottoms 1983, Carlen and Cook 1989, O'Malley 2009a, 2009b), is that money is taken for granted. Money is ubiquitous, and either it is unnoticed or it is imagined to be so prosaic it can hardly be worth theorizing. It lacks the dramatic edge of most other forms of punishment and merges almost seamlessly with bill payments of the most routine nature. This invisibility is a significant feature for a sanction in consumer societies, for mass fining generates very little of the political concern associated with mass imprisonment. But in what way are fines risk-based sanctions? As Rusche and Kirchheimer (1939) first noted many years ago, fines do not discipline individuals. They do not penetrate to the 'soul' or reform deviants. Nor is ceremonial and individualized punishment very pronounced. Fines are most frequently associated with summary forms of justice where offenders are often not even present in court, and the advance of summary justice is associated with its being linked to this 'less consequential' sanction. Indeed, courts do not even bother to make sure that the offender is the one who pays fines: it's not who pays that concerns justice, so much as that someone pays. And in the end, fines are paid without any ceremonial at all: no different to paying a bill.

Accordingly fines are not the sanction deployed where the state seeks to eliminate or condemn offences – rather, they are a sanction that seeks merely to keep the level of offending in check. In a strong sense the reason it doesn't matter who pays is that whatever the mechanism of payment it increases the costs of the unwanted action and (it is hoped) this reduces its frequency: punishing the individual wrongdoer is only one means to this end. Nowhere is this more clearly the case than in those many examples where young offenders are fined in the full knowledge that their parents will pay. In short, as Anthony Bottoms (1983) has noted, fines are 'regulatory' in Foucault's sense that they govern the frequency and distribution of unwanted actions – they reduce the probabilities of offences. They are a technique for government through risk (O'Malley 2009a).

Fines place an economic value on offending. While we frequently refer to the 'price' of crime, here this is literally the case. Like prices, to which they are very closely related, fines create what economists refer to as 'friction', making certain lines of action less attractive through increasing their monetary cost, and thereby encouraging subjects to take other options. Fines blur with other costs, notably fees to which they are often attached. In Virginia, for example, new speeding fines incorporate fees that can boost the penalty to multiple thousands of dollars, on the justification that speeding creates risks that require expensive situational prevention in the form of road engineering. This monetization of risk creates a little circuit in which risk-takers contribute to the costs of their risk-taking. Linked with digital techniques – such as occurs with vehicle barcode readers employed to detect both the usage of and speeding on freeways – fines operate as a key sanction for Deleuze's (1995) 'control societies'. Costs are levied, offences are detected, fine notices are issued, rates of offending are calculated, the need for preventative engineering is registered, and of course nowadays fines are paid – anonymously and electronically and without disrupting everyday life. Especially at the fringes of criminal offending, in ways that affect virtually all of us, fines have become a key part of the immanent control of unwanted behaviour. Just another expense of living in a commodified society.

Yet, imprisonment, a disposition imposed on a tiny minority of all offences and infringements, has attracted *all* the criminological attention: indeed, even where fines are mentioned, probably the main topic is imprisonment in default of payment. Yet it is likely that the extraordinarily high rate of imprisonment in the US is partly due to the fact that fines are much less used in criminal courts than is the case in other countries. On average, this is about a quarter as often, or less, and even then they are used very frequently in conjunction with imprisonment (O'Malley 2009a). This American exceptionalism is extraordinary considering that fines were regarded as the optimal sanction by eighteenth-century classical criminologists such as Bentham and Beccaria, and considering that the US is perhaps the most commodified of all societies. Regarding the potential of fines as a line of flight into the penological future of America, the classical criminologists' positive evaluations of money sanctions are worthy of attention.

As early as the eighteenth century, Bentham (1962 [1789]) pointed out that fines were infinitely gradable to match the seriousness of the offence. He noted that they can also operate democratically through an income-indexed tariff – so that fines can be made proportional to offenders' income or wealth. This scheme is now widely used in Scandinavia and elsewhere. Bentham regarded fines as an ideal liberal sanction because they do not take hold of the offender's body, thus minimizing coercion. Fines take away the ability to purchase pleasure, rather than solely inflicting pain. Fines do not remove offenders from the workforce and could be used to compensate those harmed by offenders. Finally, and in some ways Bentham's trump card, in the event of injustice fines can be completely restored to the wrongfully convicted, even to the point of repaying interest. I would add a further advantage of the fine. Nowadays we might add that as a sanction based upon the assumption of rational choice actors, and working through the mechanics of the commodity sector, fines operate with a criminology of the self (Garland 1996) – with very little potential to exclude or create ongoing stigmatization and disadvantage of the sort inflicted by imprisonment.

Then why are fines used so infrequently in the USA and would it be unthinkable for fines to replace prisons in degree? Two arguments are put forward by American criminologists. The first, which can be dismissed quickly, is that unlike Europe, American justice is focused on reform and thus refuses to use fines as they are not correctional (for example, Hillsman 1990). Most US jails are hardly reformatories, of course, and no evidence is presented demonstrating the implausible thesis that the American prison system is more focused on corrections than those in Britain, Australia or Germany. In addition, the fine owes its early twentieth-century resurgence in Europe to the demonstration that short terms of imprisonment are of no correctional value while expensive to the state and disruptive for society (O'Malley 2009b).

The second argument is that fines are inequitable. The Fourteenth Amendment, guaranteeing equal treatment before the law, has been used to negate fines because the possibility of imprisonment in default of payment is far greater for poor offenders than for others. Were this a serious objection, two simple techniques could settle it. First, the day-fine system, which in fact has hardly been even experimented with in the US. Second, the removal of prison as a sanction for offenders who cannot afford to pay fines (as opposed to those who refuse to pay). This is the case, for example, in Australian states such as New South Wales where, under the Fines Act, unpaid fines are passed to the State Debt Recovery Office. In the event payment is not possible over a reasonable period, the debt may be worked off by a variety of means such as unpaid work for an approved community organization or by participation in a treatment drug program. Many countries have adopted either or both options without an immediate collapse in law and order! Even in the United States, most jurisdictions long ago passed non-payment of traffic fines to civil debt collection agencies – without the consequent appearance of chaos on the roads. At the same time, fines are used, apparently satisfactorily, and prison rather rarely, to govern the hazardous domain of road safety. The much maligned Law and Economics movement (for example, Becker 1974) has long argued for fines to replace prisons. Unfortunately, American criminologists have been mute on the topic, perhaps afraid to take the risk either of being regarded as crime-friendly by the Right, or as siding with neo-liberals by the Left. But maybe the 'bad guys' have some good ideas worth taking these risks for.

For very many offences, especially of the 'risk-taking' sort – vandalism, graffiti, shoplifting, joyriding, disturbing the peace and so on – fines offer an effective risk-managerial sanction simply as pricing mechanisms. Linked to compensation orders, they also provide some means of recouping the costs of these crimes. This is already a major function of fines and related money sanctions in most jurisdictions outside the US. I would argue for their promise for *all* 'crimes without victims' including most drug offences. I would add to this all offences where the primary nature of the wrong is economic: burglary, theft, fraud, deception. Of course, where these create risks that are unacceptable (especially risks to the person) other sanctions are necessary. But even in such cases, there is no need *necessarily* for recourse to imprisonment, given the availability of non-incarcerating incapacitation. Were fines the sanction of first resort with respect to most offences in a commodity society such as the US, and were they more widely used in other jurisdictions, surely it's not so hard to envision an escape from the carceral archipelago for tens and perhaps hundreds of thousands of people.

Of course, many of the targets of criminal law are indigent people. But as suggested already, prison in default of payment is not a necessity. As Australia shows, other possibilities such as working on community programs to pay off fines have already been tried and found to function with no greater degree of difficulty than is true for the problem-ridden justice system in general. Furthermore, the model of traffic regulation provides other promising options. Fines can be seen as too permissive with respect to many risky offences. But there is no need to assume imprisonment as the necessary alternative. With respect to speeding offences, for example, there is widespread use of back-up techniques such as 'demerit points' that cumulate over a number of offences to the point at which drivers' licences are cancelled or suspended. Unlike imprisonment, the offenders' specific risk-creating capacity – rather than their general liberty – is removed. Applied to a great many offences, even offences that create risks for others, fines linked with demerit points leading ultimately to curfews, restrictions on movements associated with risk etc., seem far preferable to any form of imprisonment. Certainly, where offenders continue to offend and thus continue to create risks, imprisonment may be the last resort, at least where the risks are serious. But this form of market-based risk reduction through fines, linked with a demerit points system and some form of selective incapacitation (rather than imprisonment) may – with a little imagination – be an option that can be developed and applied to a large array of risk-creating offences.

As I keep pointing out, the problem of non-payment is always to the fore. Creating a class in debt is a major problem – but surely it is better in almost all respects than the class in prison that we have already created? And perhaps if criminologists put half the energy into thinking through such issues rather than focusing almost solely on the prison, new innovations, new monetary possibilities could be devised and promoted. And who knows, if fines were made a significant issue by criminologists in the US, maybe they would be considered officially as a viable alternative to imprisonment in that country. What exactly have we got to lose?

Fines are not the only way to go in creating a 'market for harms' in place of the carceral archipelago: another route is compensation. Again, this is not something novel, strange and hypothetical. In Japan, where fines make up 40 per cent of dispositions, another 40 per cent of cases are disposed of by requiring the offender to pay compensation to the victim. Many courts in the West are already required, or at least have the option, of issuing reparation or restitution orders in place of fines. Like the fine or any other monetary sanction, these effectively are risk-reducing or risk-spreading rather than punitive. Of course, many offenders are poor and cannot hope to repay the costs they generate. Bentham (1962/1789) knew this 200 years ago, but it did not stop him thinking about positive alternatives to prison – one such way he considered to be insurance. As with fines, it is not required that the offender always be the one to pay the monetary sanction. Even in the US, insurance schemes exist, funded by fines and fees extracted from offenders, that pay compensation to victims of crime (O'Malley 2009a: 62–5). In effect, offenders can pay their monetary penalty in the form of insurance premiums – if necessary in quite small instalments – to such a fund.

Most people already have private insurance to cover economic loss caused by crimes and need not rely on such a program. Not so the poor. Such a fines-based insurance scheme, extended and provided through an administrative system rather than the court system – which has not proven a very effective arrangement for the disbursement of crime compensation – could effectively work as an adjunct to social justice. An industry administered insurance system, funded from fines and fees, could be dedicated to compensating some of crime's economic risks – including the economic costs generated by physical injury. I would not go to the extreme voiced by Bentham (1982/1789: 572) that a crime paid for in such way almost ceases to exist. But restorative justice has already opened up a pathway with respect to a compensatory approach. Could not more active criminological exploration of the potential of wider use of monetary reparation and offender-funded insurance possibly promote a culture of compensation rather than punishment and discipline as the normal response to offending?

In this respect, as the institution of risk par excellence, insurance offers a variety of possibilities other than state-sponsored models (always likely to generate resistance, especially in the US where they are most needed). Take, for example, the high risk domain of terrorism insurance. This is imagined by Ulrich Beck (1992) to be beyond the limits of insurance mechanisms. Yet the industry, prodded into action by the state, has created innovative economic models for providing insurance in the form of terrorism bonds. This was made possible by a state interested enough in generating such economic security for its subjects in the face of terrorism (Bougen and O'Malley 2009). Where the penological imagination is stimulated, as it might be were political attention stimulated by risk-taking criminologists, a variety of similar possibilities could be innovated in order to reduce the prison population and the economic costs of crime for poor people?

Democratizing risk

It will be objected to much of the argument with respect to fines and monetary sanctions, that these 'demoralize' criminal justice. This is one of the primary criticisms of many risk-based interventions, even though it has been seen that with respect to developments such as Megan's Laws, risk can be coupled with vengeance. With respect to crimes involving physical and sexual violence, for example, it may indeed be that 'demoralization' may create limits to the use of fines. As Peter Young (1989) has argued, fining those guilty of sexual violence may well be construed as putting a market price on rape. Others have argued, against this, that were the price high enough it may well be a more effective deterrent than the relatively short periods of imprisonment some rapists receive (Becker 1974). Again, these are remarkably little explored issues and a lively debate would likely do criminology no harm.

The same is equally true for such other prominent issues as illicit drug use. It has already been suggested that there may be considerable advantages in demoralizing this offence and many similar crimes in order to minimize demonization and amplification and promote positive re-integrative measures (Young 1974). Yet even this shares risk's deceptive character. While it may appear that drug harm minimization is an 'amoral' approach, and objectionable to many on exactly these grounds, it is in fact deeply ingrained with a utilitarian morality of the least harm to the greatest number. It also carries with it an implied weighting of certain (e.g. medical) harms over other (e.g. religious) harms. As others (Latour 1994, Wynne 1996) have argued, in such ways science carries with it a concealed burden of silenced politics. We have seen various examples of this with respect to crime prevention, notably where women's concerns have been disregarded as irrational even while, arguably, they have been both empirically and experientially at least as 'valid' as those of male-centric scientific expertise. Here we seem to confront a dilemma. Are these kinds of struggle over risk irreducible, simply a matter in which opposing values create irreconcilable 'justices'? Or conversely, is it the case that a gender or value-neutral science is possible and could eventually produce 'just' prevention and risk-based justice? Both possibilities can be entertained, but it seems to me that these are not issues that can simply be resolved by fiat or technical ingenuity: again, they are deeply political. What is therefore at issue is the politicization, or better, the democratization of risk.

Elsewhere, risk theorists, such as Ulrich Beck (1992) have called for such a democratization. Confronted by a world in which, it is argued, ungoverned technological development has created risks to the entire planet, Beck calls for democratic controls to be applied to scientific growth. He sees in the 'subpolitics' of popular movements such as the Rainbow Alliance, the promise of such regulation. Existing efforts to subject 'runaway' science to democratic controls are visible in a wide variety of contexts, perhaps nowhere more clearly than with respect to the 'precautionary' politics in European law (Fisher 2008). In this there may be a lesson, for as Ewald (2002) has argued, precaution operates where the imaginable risks are too great to be chanced, yet means of calculating them are yet to be developed. A politics of precaution does not therefore stifle scientific development, so much as require research to address those problems identified as creating 'unacceptable' risks. It does not, therefore, involve the subordination of scientific findings to populist politics or to a kind of Stalinist scenario in which the truth of science is made to fit with the truth of some other regime. What would a government of crime risks look like if it were governed democratically?

One answer to this question has been the subject of experimentation by Shearing (2001) and his colleagues (Brogden and Shearing 1993, Johnston and Shearing 2003). People in the township environment in South Africa were audited on what they regarded as the main risks to their security. Perhaps surprisingly, these did not overwhelmingly relate to crime, and in some degree police were regarded as a security threat rather than a solution. Persuading the ruling ANC to redirect some of the funding for police to 'peace committees', a participatory and informal approach along the lines of restorative justice was established in which communities addressed the resolution of conflicts that threatened security. In this risk-oriented environment, Shearing notes that 'justice' took on a rather different meaning from that familiar to courts. While the procedures strongly resembled restorative justice, justice was not so much about the backward-looking moral condemnation of offenders, the attribution of blame and the delivery of punishment. Rather people focused on forward-looking questions of risk – on the attempt to ensure that unwanted events and actions did not happen again. In this much, the movement took some of its momentum from the broader political environment of 'truth and reconciliation' that characterized South African politics after the collapse of apartheid. Crime prevention was being reshaped as a democratic process of risk reduction.

As a model for democratizing risk, this seems to have considerable possibilities for so-called developed societies, especially given the fact that restorative justice has already achieved a considerable purchase in criminal justice countries such as Britain, Canada and Australia. Together with advocates of restorative justice, Shearing seeks to 'empower' communities (latterly in Argentina and Northern Ireland) by handing over to them many crime and security problems. This privileges government by communities in ways that echo parallel emphases in neo-liberal governance, evoking a 'customer' oriented framework. Indeed, Shearing refers to 'markets in security' in this respect. His approach also appropriates other neo-liberal modes and rhetorics of governance in which communities take control of their own problems, something key neo-liberal commentators regard as providing superior services to those offered by experts (Osborne and Gaebler 1993). This marginalization or even exclusion of experts is equally a characteristic of restorative justice, to which Shearing's democratization of risk clearly owes much. Perhaps this would also warm the cockles of Beck's anti-expert heart. But is even this the optimal way to approach democratization of crime risks?

Expertise and the democratization of risk

One reason for excluding expertise is the tendency of expert knowledge to trump lay knowledge because of the authority attributed to its bearers. This has been the experience, for example, where police are involved in local neighbourhood crime prevention organizations, and clearly it is also the case with medical expertise in drug harm minimization programs. In both cases, generalized knowledge is given authoritative 'objective' status, while local or experiential knowledge is reduced to the status merely of 'subjective' impressions. This distinction has been exposed to considerable critique. Bryan Wynne (1996) for example, has shown that even in highly arcane areas such as nuclear contamination, local knowledge of risks may prove more accurate because expert knowledge is abstracted and general. Scientific expertise brings with it the strength of theoretical analysis, and also knowledge of general patterns against which to understand the local. But at the same time such abstract-general knowledge suffers from the fact that it has a less acute grasp of the complexity and particularity of the local situation. Furthermore, the concerns of experts may not match the security and risk concerns of the locals. Wynne (1996: 61) suggests that this raises a 'potentially epistemological conflict with science about the underlying purpose of knowledge … but also about the extent to which scientific knowledge is open to substantive criticism and improvement or correction by lay people'.

In the field of crime risks, these issues have been seen in several contexts already. Many women's experience of the significance of crime risks do not tally with those of largely male experts because women's perceptions of risk are overlaid with fears of sexual assault. Likewise, the elderly appear 'irrationally' afraid of crime because they are aware that the consequences of physical assault are likely to be much more severe for them than for a younger person. Women object to crime prevention advice to avoid public places at night not because they are unaware of the risks, but because they object to this gendered restriction placed on them by the failure of the state to provide security against specifically male violence. Increased policing in risky areas may be opposed by residents not because they under-estimate the real risks of crime but because they are more concerned that the increased police presence increases the risk that their children will be targeted. In such cases, both parties may be empirically correct, but the 'facts' are heavily imbued with value differences. This is even more clear with different evaluations of what constitutes a 'serious' risk, differences of opinion over which risks should be prioritized, differences over what is a 'reasonable' measure to adopt in order to reduce risks and so on. In this respect there is clearly the necessity for a politics of risk.

In contrast to the position adopted in much restorative and 'participatory' justice, this does not imply keeping experts out, but rather necessitates exposing governing authorities to critique and evaluation from those who are regarded as at risk and are to be the subjects of risk-based government. Even so, one of the important issues this overlooks is that differences *within* each category tend to be minimized. In fields such as crime prevention and risk-based justice there is rarely one monolithic set of expertise, as may be illustrated with respect to the now familiar field of drug harm minimization. Youth drug workers and police often do not see eye-to-eye, while the perspectives of health professionals and police are also frequently at odds. Strained relations emerge between 'community' police and police adhering to the crime fighting model. Add to this the involvement of probation officers, local council workers, elected council officials representing diverse wards and so on, and the mix becomes more unstable and contested. A democratization of risk thus has to democratize relations *between* 'experts'.

While this may appear just to create yet another level of politics, it can also help break down one of the more enduring reasons given for excluding 'expertise' by challenging the authority of a monolithic knowledge. The same, of course, applies to the 'lay' knowledges. In many, if not most fields of crime risk, there will be differences of experience and opinion among those 'at risk' (including whether or not they are 'at risk'). And some of the greatest difficulties and most adventurous possibilities in this respect are created by the almost taken-for-granted binary of victims and offenders.

Victims, offenders and risky justice

Setting up a binary of victims and offenders is always tempting in a politics of crime risk, especially where the offenders are deeply unpopular. It is difficult not to do this with many sexual and violent predatory offences. Yet if we take seriously the idea that justice is to be about reducing and democratizing risks, this is an unpleasant pill – especially so for victims – that must be swallowed. The voice and the knowledge of these offenders, their participation and even enlistment has to be considered – or at least debated. Again Third World countries such as the Rwandan *gacacas* courts dealing with genocidieres may show us the lead, to create a justice where, no matter how difficult, the future takes precedence over the past. But maybe it is also necessary to move beyond victim–offender binaries altogether in democratizing risk?

Examples of sexual violence and serious physical violence no doubt are too difficult for such an exercise to cut its teeth on. But there are many other risky crimes where this approach can be, and in some jurisdictions has been, mobilized. Certainly illicit drug use, as a massive problem for criminal justice almost everywhere, provides a more tractable but still contentious case. Despite the idea that these are crimes without victims, the politics of illicit drug crimes are so contentious precisely because many – on both sides – feel victimized. In this respect, perhaps another borrowing from neo-liberals, creating another line of flight in criminal justice, is drug harm minimization's tendency to adopt a language of stakeholders in place of victim-offender binaries. First it allows conflicts of interest to be centered, rather than assuming that one party is necessarily in the right and the other to be shamed. Second, it allows 'victims', 'offenders', 'experts' and others to engage in an exchange that recognizes possibilities of conflict. Recognition of the existence and even centrality of conflicts of interest is important because – contrary to the imagery of the 'community' as deployed in restorative justice – it allows for diversity of values within the community concerned. In this way, such an approach avoids the problem identified by George Pavlich (2005) that an assumption of communal consensus in restorative justice creates a potential for 'totalitarian' domination: one set of values and experiences are to be the subject of condemnation, denial and apology. While no doubt this is sometimes defensible (for example, with sexual assault), its ethical and political dangers are clear. First it may regard problems as problems created by bad individuals rather than systemic problems – such as the question of the place of women and the nature of sexuality in social relations more generally. Second, it may ignore or suppress social diversity and sometimes social conflicts of a sort that it is important for 'the community' to recognize, and come to terms with. These are questions of justice, but not of individual justice (O'Malley 2008).

Precisely because it sets up a victim-offender binary, and by so doing prioritizes rectification of past wrongs by one party, restorative justice is rather poorly equipped at present to deal with such matters. Much the same is true for the local preventative justice hearings promoted by Shearing. With a stakeholder politics we move from dispute resolution and adjudication, where only one party is right, toward the possibility of dispute management. Thus the interests of drug users on the streets and of the shopkeepers who find the presence of users bad for business, are not reduced to a scenario in which the shopkeepers are assumed to be in the right because they have suffered harms. Such a scenario more or less explicitly coerces drug users to conform, or move to another area. It puts no obligation on shopkeepers (or anyone else) to do anything about the plight of users, or to reconsider their own attitudes and practices. This is even more so where, as in most restorative programs, the offender is required to acknowledge the offence as a condition of entering the program. A stakeholder politics on the other hand sets up a process of negotiation. This would seem especially to offer promise where 'offending' is linked to situations in which community responses may imply a potentially repressive consensus – such as racially or ethnically diverse settings, or culture clashes between generations or subcultures (such as drug subcultures). It is also possible that crime prevention is effected in some degree simply through the increased tolerance for differences and the erosion of criminalization was a way of governing risks and harms.

Conclusions: The impossibility theorem and risky justice

Much of what has been written above will be discarded as naive, if only because in a culture of control the likelihood of such proposals being acted upon is low. They are also rather vague and general – and in many ways not even novel – for I am not here attempting to provide a new program so much as a stimulus for further experimentation. Throughout this book, I have pointed to the importance of seeing exceptions to any presumed hegemony of a culture of control as worth seizing on; as opportunities for something different. I have also argued that it is worth recognizing that neo-liberals themselves put forward a number of techniques and discourses – of stakeholders, markets, monetization, enterprise, even of embracing risk, that can and should be taken seriously and exploited rather than ignored or rejected as shams.

It is not my intention to minimize the significance of the problems confronting democratization of risk and experimentation with risk-based justice in the mainstream of criminal justice. However, recognition of significant obstacles need not imply inaction. As I have argued elsewhere (O'Malley 2008) the sites in which experimentation should begin are not necessarily at the state or national level where rationalities and techniques containing or regulating experimentation are well established. Regional and local or municipal government is far more variable, especially in traditionally 'Left' areas. In many places people have not experienced whatever real or illusory benefits the punitive turn may have delivered to others, and may provide a receptive environment for experiments at the local level. 'Problem' public housing areas offer such opportunities for experiments where residents' associations take their own initiatives in response to perceived victimization of their young people by the criminal justice system.

Also, it is important in this respect to remember that 'security' is not only about crime, as Shearing's pioneering work in South African townships revealed. If residents are given opportunities and resources with which to define and act upon their perceptions and local knowledges of security and risk, then unanticipated opportunities for productive interventions may open up. These do not have to confront the ranks of law and order enforcers and technocrats but instead can work in the spaces they leave vacant. Opportunism is the name of this game; it is a resource for the weak, such as criminologists. Rather than despairing, we need to attend to finding the gaps and fault lines, the sites of resistance and the places or issues where discontent with current programs (or their absence) prevails.

Maybe this is sidestepping the 'real' issues by failing to confront the criminal justice system head-on. Yet if indeed the culture of control and popular punitivism are as hegemonic as some criminologists would have us believe, then there is little point in directly confronting the state and we may need to look elsewhere. After all, significant changes in criminal justice have come from interventions in apparently marginal sites. John Braithwaite's hugely influential approach to reintegrative justice grew very largely from such beginnings in the small rural Australian town of Wagga Wagga where only low ranking police officers were involved. Shearing's work was carried out in Third World townships. The point is not whether one likes or dislikes the approach taken by Shearing or of any brand of restorative or re-integrative justice. It is that these illustrate examples of opportunistic innovation that opened up new directions and took 'justice' away from a punitive line. Such work pursued lines of flight that could offer an alternative to the present. To repeat, lines of flight are in their nature dangerous: any change we advocate may be co-opted and may open up developments that have unanticipated negative consequences. But to argue that this is inevitable should make us question the point of our 'critical' discipline. Nothing is more disempowering than theoretically driven pessimism. A risk-taking criminology may just be a better alternative.

bibliography

Agamben, G. (2000) *Means Without End*. Chicago: University of Chicago Press.

Agamben, G. (2005) *State of Exception*. University of Chicago Press.

Aharoni, Y. (1984) *The No-Risk Society*. New York: Basic Books.

Andrews, D. and Bonta, J. (2006) 'The recent past and near future of risk/need assessment'. *Crime and Delinquency* 52: 7–27.

Andrews, D. and Dowden, C. (2007) 'The risk-need-responsivity model of assessment and human service in prevention and corrections'. *Canadian Journal of Criminology and Criminal Justice* 49: 439–64.

Ashworth, A. and Zedner, L. (forthcoming) 'Just prevention. Preventive justice and the limits of the criminal law'. In S. Green and A. Duff (eds.) *The Philosophical Foundations of Criminal Law*.

Austin, J., Clark, J., Hardyman, P. and Henry, D. (1999) 'The impact of three strikes and you're out'. *Punishment and Society* 1: 131–62.

Batchelor, S. (2007) '"Getting mad wi' it": risk-seeking by young women'. In K. Hannah-Moffat and P. O'Malley (eds.) *Gendered Risks*. London: Glasshouse Press. pp. 205–29.

Baker, T. and Simon, J. (eds.) (2002) *Embracing Risk*. Chicago: University of Chicago Press.

Bauman, Z. (2000) 'Social issues of law and order'. *British Journal of Criminology* 40: 205–21.

Beck, U. (1992) *Risk Society: Toward a New Modernity*. New York: Sage.

Beck, U. (1997) *World Risk Society*. London: Polity Press.

Beck, U. (2002) 'The terrorist threat: world risk society revisited'. *Theory, Culture and Society* 19: 39–55.

Becker, G. (1974) 'Crime and punishment: an economic approach'. In G. Becker and W. Landes (eds.) *Essays in the Economics of Crime and Punishment*. New York: Columbia University Press. pp. 27–36.

Bentham, J. (1962) [1789] 'Principals of penal law'. In J. Bowring (ed.) *The Works of Jeremy Bentham Vol. I*. New York: Russell and Russell. pp. 365–580.

Bentham, J. (1982) [1789] *An Introduction to the Principles of Morals and Legislation*. (ed. J. Burns and H.L.A. Hart) London: Methuen.

Berman, M. (1983) *All that is Solid Melts into Air*. London: Verso.

Bloomenfeld, M. (2007) 'Introduction: sentencing at risk'. *Canadian Journal of Criminology and Criminal Justice* 49: 431–4.

Bottoms, A. (1983) 'Some neglected features of contemporary penal systems'. In D. Garland and P. Young (eds.) *The Power to Punish*. London: Heinemann.

Bougen, P. and O'Malley, P. (2009) 'Bureaucracy, imagination and US domestic security policy'. *Security Journal* 22: 101–18.

Brogden, M. and Shearing, C. (1993) *Policing for a New South Africa*. London: Routledge.

Burgess, E. (1928) 'Factors making for success of failure on parole'. *Journal of Criminal Law and Criminology* 19: 239–306.

Burgess, E. (1936) 'Protecting the public by parole and parole prediction'. *Journal of Criminal Law and Criminology* 27: 491–502.

Campbell, E. (2004) 'Police narrativity in the risk society'. *British Journal of Criminology* 44: 695–714.

Carlen, P. and Cook, D. (eds.) (1989) *Paying for Crime*. Milton Keynes: Open University Press.

Cohen, S. (1979) 'The punitive city: notes on the dispersal of social control'. *Contemporary Crises* 3: 339–63.

Cohen, S. (1985) *Visions of Social Control*. London: Polity Press.

Colquhoun, P. (1796) *A Treatise on the Police of the Metropolis* (2nd edn.). London: H. Fry.

Cross, G. (1993) *Time and Money. The Making of Consumer Culture*. London: Routledge.

CPCC (Crime Prevention Council of Canada) (1997) *Preventing Crime by Investing in Families*. Ottawa: NCPC.

Cullen, F. (2005) 'The twelve people who saved rehabilitation: how the science of criminology made a difference'. *Criminology* 43: 1–42.

de Certeau, M. (1985) *The Practice of Everyday Life*. Berkeley: University of California Press.

Deleuze, G. (1995) 'Postscript on control societies'. In G. Deleuze (ed.) *Negotiations 1972–1990*. New York: Columbia University Press. pp. 177–82.

Denton, B. (2001) *Dealing. Women in the Drug Economy*. Sydney: University of New South Wales Press.

Dixon, D. (1991) *From Prohibition to Regulation. Bookmaking, Anti-Gambling and the Law*. Oxford: Clarendon Press.

Douglas, M. (1992) *Risk and Blame. Essays in Cultural Theory*. London: Routledge.

Downes, D. and Davies, B. (1976) *Gambling, Work and Leisure: A Study Across Three Areas*. London: Routledge & Kegan Paul.

Duster, T. (1990) *Backdoor to Eugenics*. London: Routledge.

Ericson, R. and Haggerty, K. (1998) *Policing the Risk Society*. Toronto: University of Toronto Press.

Everingham, S. (1998) 'Benefits and costs of early childhood interventions'. In Parliament of NSW (ed.) *Crime Prevention Through Social Support*. Sydney: Parliament of NSW Legislative Council. pp. 131–47.

Ewald, F. (2002) 'The return of Descarte's malicious demon. An outline of a philosophy of precaution'. In T. Baker and J. Simon (eds.) *Embracing Risk*. Chicago: University of Chicago Press. pp. 273–301.

Eysenck, H. (1978) *Crime and Personality*. London: Paladin.

Featherstone, M. (1994) *Consumer Culture and Postmodernism*. London: Sage.

Feeley, M. and Simon, J. (1992) 'The new penology: notes on the emerging strategy of corrections and its implications'. *Criminology* 30: 449–74.

Feeley, M. and Simon, J. (1994) 'Actuarial justice: the emerging new criminal law'. In D. Nelken (ed.) *The Futures of Criminology*. New York: Sage. pp. 173–201.

Ferrell, J., Hayward, K., Morrison, W. and Presdee, M. (eds.) (2004) *Cultural Criminology Unleashed*. London: Glasshouse Press.

Fisher, E. (2008) *Risk Regulation and Administrative Constitutionalism*. Oxford: Hart.

Freiberg, A. (2000) 'Guerillas in our midst? Judicial responses to governing the dangerous'. In M. Brown and J. Pratt (eds.) *Dangerous Offenders. Punishment and Social Order*. London: Routledge. pp. 51–70.

Friedman, M. (1994) 'The War on Drugs as a socialist enterprise'. In T. Szasz and M. Friedman (eds.) *On Liberty and Drugs*. Washington. The Drug Policy Foundation.

Garland, D. (1985) *Punishment and Welfare: A History of Penal Strategies*. Aldershot: Ashgate.

Garland, D. (1991) *Punishment and Modern Society*. Oxford: Oxford University Press.

Garland, D. (1996) 'The limits of the sovereign state: strategies of crime control in contemporary society'. *British Journal of Criminology* 36: 445–71.

Garland, D. (2001) *The Culture of Control*. Oxford: Oxford University Press.

Giddens, A. (1994) 'Living in a post-traditional society'. In U. Beck, A. Giddens and S. Lasch (eds.) *Reflexive Modernisation. Politics, Tradition and Aesthetics in the Modern Social Order*. London: Polity Press. pp. 56–109.

Gilling, D. (1997) *Crime Prevention. Theory, Policy and Politics*. London: UCL Press.

Glaser, D. (1962) 'Prediction tables as accounting devices for judges and parole boards'. *Crime and Delinquency* 8: 239–58.

Glaser, D. (1985) 'Who gets probation and parole: case study versus actuarial decision making'. *Crime and Delinquency* 31: 367–78.

Glueck, S. and Glueck, E. (1946) *After-Conduct of Discharged Offenders*. New York: Macmillan.

Greenberg, D. (2002) 'Striking out in democracy'. *Punishment and Society* 4: 237–52.

Hall, S., Winlow, S. and Ancrum, C. (2008) *Criminal Identities and Consumer Culture. Crime, Exclusion and the New Culture of Narcissism*. Devon: Willan.

Halliday, T. (2004) *Rescuing Business. The Making of Corporate Bankruptcy Law in England and the United States*. Oxford: Oxford University Press.

Halsey, M. (2008) 'Narrating the chase: edgework and young people's experiences of crime'. In T. Anthony and C. Cuneen (eds.) *The Critical Criminology Companion*. Sydney: Hawksworth Press. pp. 105–17.

Hannah-Moffat, K. (1999) 'Moral agent or actuarial subject. Risk and Canadian women's imprisonment'. *Theoretical Criminology* 3: 71–95.

Hannah-Moffat, K. (2005) 'Criminogenic needs and the transformative risk subject'. *Punishment and Society* 7: 29–51.

Hannah-Moffat, K. and O'Malley, P. (2007) 'Gendered risk: an introduction'. In K. Hannah-Moffat and P. O'Malley (eds.) *Gendered Risks*. London: Glasshouse Press. pp. 1–30.

Hayward, K. (2004) *City Limits. Crime, Consumer Culture and the Urban Experience.* London: Glasshouse Press.

Hayward, K. and Hobbs, D. (2007) 'Beyond the binge in "booze Britain": market-led liminalization and the spectacle of binge drinking'. *British Journal of Sociology* 58: 437–56.

Hebenton, B. and Thomas, T. (1996) 'Sexual offenders in the community: reflections of problems of law, community and risk management in the USA, England and Wales'. *International Journal of the Sociology of Law* 24: 427–43.

Hillsman, S. (1990) 'Fines and day fines'. *Crime and Justice. A Review of Research* 12: 50–98.

Homel, R. (1998) 'Pathways to prevention'. In Parliament of NSW (ed.) *Crime Prevention Through Social Support.* Sydney: Parliament of NSW Legislative Council. pp. 91–100.

Horwitz, M. (1977) *The Transformation of American Law.* Harvard: Harvard University Press.

Hudson, F. (1974) 'Crime prevention – past and present'. *Security Gazette* 1974: 292–95 and 332–33.

Hutchinson, S. (2006) 'Countering catastrophe: reform, punishment and the modern liberal response'. *Punishment and Society* 8: 443–67.

Jackson-Jacobs, C. (2004) 'Taking a beating: the narrative gratification of fighting as an underdog'. In J. Ferrell, K. Hayward, W. Morrison and M. Presdee (eds.) *Cultural Criminology Unleashed.* London: Glasshouse Press. pp. 231–45.

Jefferson, T. and Walker, M. (1992) 'Ethnic minorities in the criminal justice system', *Criminal Law Review* 1992: 83–8.

Johnston, L. (2000) *Policing Britain. Risk, Security and Governance.* London: Routledge.

Johnston, L. and Shearing, C. (2003) *Governing Security. Explorations in Policing and Justice.* London: Routledge.

Katz, J. (1988) *The Seductions of Crime.* New York: Basic Books.

Kerr, P. (1996) *A Philosophical Investigation.* Harmondsworth: Penguin.

Kemshall, H. (1998) *Risk in Probation Practice.* Aldershot: Dartmouth.

Kemshall, H. (2003) *Understanding Risk in the Criminal Justice System.* Milton Keynes: Open University Press.

Latour, B. (1994) *We have Never Been Modern.* Cambridge Mass.: Harvard University Press.

Levi, R. (2000) 'The mutuality of risk and community: the adjudication of community notification statutes'. *Economy and Society* 29: 578–601.

Lupton, D. (1999) *Risk.* London: Routledge. (Especially Chapter 3. Risk and Culture.)

Lyng, S. (1991) 'Edgework: a social psychological analysis of voluntary risk taking'. *American Journal of Sociology* 95: 887–921.

Lyng, S. (ed.) (2005) *Edgework. The Sociology of Risk Taking*. London: Routledge.

Mannheim, H. and Wilkins, L. (1955) *Prediction Methods in Relation to Borstal Training*. London: HMSO.

Martinson, R. (1974) 'What works? Questions and answers about prison reform'. *The Public Interest* 25.

Matza, D. (1964) *Delinquency and Drift*. New York: Wiley.

Maurutto, P. and Hannah-Moffat, K. (2007) 'Understanding risk in the context of the Youth Criminal Justice Act'. *Canadian Journal of Criminology and Criminal Justice* 49: 465–92.

Measham, F. (2004) 'Drug and alcohol research. The case for cultural criminology'. In J. Ferrell, K. Hayward, W. Morrison and M. Presdee (eds.) *Cultural Criminology Unleashed*. London: Glasshouse Press. pp. 207–18.

Merton, R. (1938) *Social Structure and Anomie*. Glencoe: The Free Press.

Miller, E. (1991) 'Assessing the risk of inattention to class, race/ethnicity and gender: comment on Lyng'. *American Journal of Sociology* 96: 1530–4.

Miller, W. (1958) 'Lower class culture as a generating milieu of gang delinquency'. *Journal of Social Issues* 14: 5–19.

Miller, W.J. (2005) 'Adolescents on the edge. The sensual side of delinquency'. In S. Lyng (ed.) *Edgework. The Sociology of Risk Taking*. London: Routledge. pp. 153–72.

NCP (National Crime Prevention) (1999) *Pathways to Prevention. Developmental and Early Intervention Approaches to Crime in Australia*. Canberra: Commonwealth Attorney General's Department.

Nelkin, D. and Lindee, M. (1995) *The DNA Mystique: The Gene as a Cultural Icon*. New York: Freeman.

Ohlin, L. (1951) *Selection for Parole*. New York: Russell Sage Foundation.

O'Malley, P. (1991) 'Legal networks and domestic security'. *Studies in Law, Politics and Society* 11: 165–84.

O'Malley, P. (1992) 'Risk, power and crime prevention'. *Economy and Society* 21: 252–75.

O'Malley, P. (2000) 'Uncertain subjects. Risk, liberalism and contract'. *Economy and Society* 29: 460–84.

O'Malley, P. (2003) 'The uncertain promise of risk'. *The Australian and New Zealand Journal of Criminology* 37: 323–43.

O'Malley, P. (2004) *Risk, Uncertainty and Government*. London: Glasshouse Press.

O'Malley, P. (2008) 'Experiments in risk and criminal justice'. *Theoretical Criminology* 12: 451–70.

O'Malley, P. (2009a) *The Currency of Justice. Fines and Damages in Consumer Societies*. London: Glasshouse Press.

O'Malley, P. (2009b) 'Theorizing fines'. *Punishment and Society* 11: 67–83.

O'Malley, P. and Hutchinson, S. (2007) 'Reinventing prevention. Why did "crime prevention" develop so late?'. *British Journal of Criminology* 47: 439–54.

O'Malley, P. and Mugford, S. (1992) 'Moral technology: the political agenda of random drug testing'. *Social Justice* 18: 122–46.

O'Malley, P. and Mugford, S. (1994) 'Crime, excitement and modernity'. In G. Barak (ed.) *Varieties of Criminology*. Westport: Praeger. pp. 189–212.

O'Malley, P. and Palmer, D. (1996) 'Post-Keynesian policing'. *Economy and Society* 25: 137–55.

O'Malley, P. and Valverde, M. (2004) 'Pleasure, freedom and drugs. The uses of "pleasure" in liberal governance of drug and alcohol consumption'. *Sociology* 38: 25–42.

Osborne, T. and Gaebler, T. (1993) *Reinventing Government. How the Entrepreneurial Spirit is Transforming the Public Sector*. New York: Plume Books.

Pavlich, G. (2005) *Governing Paradoxes of Restorative Justice*. London: Cavendish Press.

Pratt, J. (2006) *Penal Populism*. New York: Sage.

Pratt, J., Brown, D., Brown, M., Hallsworth, S. and Morrison, W. (eds.) (2005) *The New Punitiveness. Trends, Theories and Perspectives*. Devon: Willan.

Presdee, M. (2000) *Cultural Criminology and the Carnival of Crime*. London: Routledge.

Race, K. (2007) 'Engaging in a culture of barebacking: gay men and the risk of HIV protection'. In K. Hannah-Moffat and P. O'Malley (eds.) *Gendered Risks*. London: Glasshouse Press. pp. 99–126.

Rafter, N. (2008) *The Criminal Brain. Understanding Biological Theories of Crime*. New York: New York University Press.

Rajah, V. (2007) 'Resistance as edgework in violent intimate relationships of drug-involved women'. *British Journal of Criminology* 47: 196–213.

Rand Corporation (1998) *Diverting Children from a Life of Crime*. Washington, DC: Rand Corporation.

Reichman, N. (1986) 'Managing crime risks: toward an insurance based model of social control'. *Research in Law and Social Control* 8: 151–72.

Reith, G. (2005) 'On the edge. Drugs and the consumption of risk in late modernity'. In S. Lyng (ed.) *Edgework. The Sociology of Risk Taking*. London: Routledge. pp. 227–46.

Rhodes, T. (1997) 'Risk theory in epidemic times. Sex, drugs and the social organization of risk behaviour', *Sociology of Health and Illness* 19: 208–27.

Robinson, G. (2008) 'Late modern rehabilitation'. *Punishment and Society* 10: 429–45.

Rose, N. (1996) 'The death of the "social"? Refiguring the territory of government'. *Economy and Society* 25: 327–56.

Rose, N. (1999) *Powers of Freedom: Reframing Political Thought*. Cambridge: Cambridge University Press.

Rose, N. (2000) 'The biology of culpability. Pathological identity and crime control in a biological culture'. *Theoretical Criminology* 4: 5–34.

Rose, N. (2008) *The Politics of Life Itself*. Princeton: Princeton University Press.

Rose, N., O'Malley, P. and Valverde, M. (2006) 'Governmentality'. *Annual Review of Law and Social Science* 2: 83–104.

Rosenbaum, M. (1981) *Women on Heroin*. New Jersey: Rutgers University Press.

Rusche, G. and Kirchheimer, O. (1939) *Punishment and Social Structure*. New York: Columbia University Press.

Shearing, C. (2001) 'Transforming security. A South African experiment'. In H. Strang and J. Braithwaite (eds.) *Restorative Justice and Civil Society*. Cambridge: Cambridge University Press. pp. 15–34.

Shearing, S. and Stenning, P. (1985) 'From panopticon to Disneyland: the development of discipline'. In A. Doob and E. Greenspan (eds.) *Perspectives in Criminal Law*. Toronto: Canada Law Book Co.

Simmel, G. (1990 [1895]) *The Philosophy of Money* (enlarged edition). New York: Routledge.

Simon, J. (1988) 'The ideological effects of actuarial practices'. *Law and Society Review* 22: 771–800.

Simon, J. (1998) 'Managing the monstrous. Sex offenders and the new penology'. *Psychology, Public Policy and Law* 4: 452–67.

Simon, J. (2002) 'Taking risks: extreme sports and the embrace of risk in advanced liberal societies'. In T. Baker and J. Simon (eds.) *Embracing Risk*. Chicago University Press. pp. 177–208.

Simon, J. and Feeley, M. (1995) 'True crime. The new penology and public discourse on crime'. In T. Blomberg and S. Cohen (eds.) *Law, Punishment and Social Control: Essays in Honor of Sheldon Messinger*. New York: Aldine de Gruyter. pp. 147–80.

Smith, C. (2005) 'Financial edgework. Trading in market currents'. In S. Lyng (ed.) *Edgework. The Sociology of Risk Taking*. London: Routledge. pp. 187–202.

Stanko, E. (1996) 'When precaution is normal: a feminist critique of crime prevention'. In L. Gelsthorpe and A. Morris (eds.) *Feminist Perspectives in Criminology*. Milton Keynes: Open University Press. pp. 123–48.

Stenson, K. and Watt, P. (1999) 'Governmentality and "the death of the social"?: A discourse analysis of local government texts in south-east England'. *Urban Studies* 36: 189–201.

Thatcher, M. (1992) *The Downing Street Years*. London: Harper Collins.

Tolley, S. and Tregeagle, S. (1998) 'Children's family centres. Integrated support services to prevent abuse and neglect of children'. In Standing Committee of Law and Justice (ed.) *Crime Prevention Through Social Support*. Sydney: Parliament of New South Wales Legislative Council. pp. 83–90.

Vaaranen, H. (2004) 'Stories from the streets: some fieldwork notes on the seduction of speed'. In J. Ferrell, K. Hayward, W. Morrison and M. Presdee (eds.) *Cultural Criminology Unleashed*. London: Glasshouse Press. pp. 244–8.

Walklate, S. (1997) 'Risk and criminal victimisation: a modernist dilemma?'. *British Journal of Criminology* 37: 235–46.

Ward, T. and Maruna, S. (2007) *Rehabilitation: Beyond the Risk Paradigm*. New York: Routledge.

White, G. (2003) *Tort Law in America. An Intellectual History* (expanded edition). Oxford: Oxford University Press.

Winlow, S. and Hall, S. (2006) *Violent Night: Urban Leisure and Contemporary Culture*. New York: Berg.

Wynne, B. (1996) 'May the sheep safely graze? A reflexive view of the expert-lay knowledge divide'. In S. Lash and B. Wynne (eds.) *Risk, Environment and Modernity*. New York: Sage. pp. 44–83.

Young, J. (1974) *The Drugtakers*. St Albans: Paladin.

Young, J. (1999) *The Exclusive Society. Social Exclusion, Crime and Difference in Late Modernity*. New York: Sage.

Young, J. (2007) *The Vertigo of Late Modernity*. New York: Sage.

Young, P. (1989) 'Punishment, money and a sense of justice'. In P. Carlen and D. Cook (eds.) *Paying for Crime*. Milton Keynes: Open University Press.

Zedner, L. (2009) *Security*. London: Routledge.

index

self-fulfilment 68–71, 75
sex-offender laws 4, 12, 16, 32–3, 91
Shearing, Clifford 92–3, 98, 99
Shield of Confidence Home
    Security Program (Canada) 30
shoplifting 62, 64
short-term hedonism 7, 59–60, 70
silent policemen 29
Simmel, Georg 21, 69
Simon, Jonathan
    see also embracing risk (Baker
        and Simon)
    actuarial justice 5, 42–8
    on imprisonment 22
    on risk-taking 14, 71, 84
    on sex-offender laws 16, 33
situational crime prevention
    29–30, 32
South Africa 92–3, 98, 99
state of exception (Agamben) 5–6
statistics 2, 27–8, 29
    see also actuarial justice/new
        penology (Feeley and
        Simon)
street car racing 21–2, 73
street fighting/robbery 62–3
subterranean risk-taking 9, 14,
    73–4
surveillance 29

taxes on cigarettes 20
Thatcher, Margaret 20
Thomas, Terry 12
'three strikes and you're out'
    legislation 4, 5, 44–5
thrill seeking 7, 22

victims 95–7

Walklate, Sandra 75–6, 77
War on Drugs 13–4, 34–6, 84
Ward, Tony 51
welfare state 23–5
'What Works' (Martinson) 23–5
    see also risk-needs-responsivity
        (RNR)
white-collar crimes 73–4
Wilkins, Leslie T. 46
women 27–8, 49–50, 51, 75–7, 94
    see also sex offender laws
workhouses 56
Wynne, Bryan 94

'yoke of foresight' (Bentham) 55
Young, Jock 5, 66
Young, Peter 91

zero tolerance policing
    (ZTP) 31–2

Available in the Compact Criminology series.

crime and human rights
Joachim J. Savelsberg

crime and risk
Pat O'Malley

comparative criminal justice
David Nelken

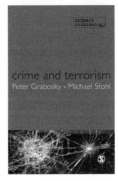

crime and terrorism
Peter Grabosky • Michael Stohl

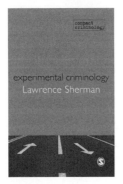

experimental criminology
Lawrence Sherman